Contents

Table of Cases

Table of Statutes

Table of Statutory Instruments

Table of Legislation

How to use this book

Welcome to this new edition of Routledge English Legal System Lawcards. In response to student feedback, we've added some new features to these new editions to give you all the support and preparation you need in order to face your law exams with confidence.

Inside this book you will find:

■ NEW tables of cases and statutes for ease of reference

■ Revision Checklists

We've summarised the key topics you will need to know for your law exams and broken them down into a handy revision checklist. Check them out at the beginning of each chapter, then after you have the chapter down, revisit the checklist and tick each topic off as you gain knowledge and confidence.

Sources of law

1

Primary legislation: Acts of Parliament	■
Secondary legislation	■
Case law	■
System of precedent	■
Common law	■
Equity	■
EU law	■
Human Rights Act 1998	■

▦ Key Cases

We've identified the key cases that are most likely to come up in exams. To help you to ensure that you can cite cases with ease, we've included a brief account of the case and judgment for a quick aide-memoire.

HENDY LENNOX v GRAHAME PUTTICK [1984]

Basic facts

Diesel engines were supplied, subject to a *Romalpa* clause, then fitted to generators. Each engine had a serial number. When the buyer became insolvent the seller sought to recover one engine. The Receiver argued that the process of fitting the engine to the generator passed property to the buyer. The court disagreed and allowed the seller to recover the still identifiable engine despite the fact that some hours of work would be required to disconnect it.

Relevance

If the property remains identifiable and is not irredeemably changed by the manufacturing process a *Romalpa* clause may be viable.

▦ Companion Website

At the end of each chapter you will be prompted to visit the Routledge Lawcards companion website where you can test your understanding online with specially prepared multiple-choice questions, as well as revise the key terms with our online glossary.

You should now be confident that you would be able to tick all of the boxes on the checklist at the beginning of this chapter. To check your knowledge of Sources of law why not visit the companion website and take the Multiple Choice Question test. Check your understanding of the terms and vocabulary used in this chapter with the flashcard glossary.

▣ Exam Practice

Once you've acquired the basic knowledge, you'll want to put it to the test. The Routledge Questions and Answers provides examples of the kinds of questions that you will face in your exams, together with suggested answer plans and a fully-worked model answer. We've included one example free at the end of this book to help you put your technique and understanding into practice.

QUESTION 1

What are the main sources of law today?

Answer plan

This is, apparently, a very straightforward question, but the temptation is to ignore the European Community (EU) as a source of law and to over-emphasise custom as a source. The following structure does not make these mistakes:

▣ in the contemporary situation, it would not be improper to start with the EU as a source of UK law;

▣ then attention should be moved on to domestic sources of law: statute and common law;

▣ the increased use of delegated legislation should be emphasised;

▣ custom should be referred to, but its extremely limited operation must be emphasised.

ANSWER

European law

Since the UK joined the European Economic Community (EEC), now the EU, it has progressively but effectively passed the power to create laws which are operative in this country to the wider European institutions. The UK is now subject to Community law, not just as a direct consequence of the various treaties of accession passed by the UK Parliament, but increasingly, it is subject to the secondary legislation generated by the various institutions of the EU.

Sources of law

1

The law in England and Wales is derived from a number of different sources. The two main sources are statute (Acts of Parliament) and case law.

STATUTE

PRIMARY LEGISLATION

Parliament is responsible for making legislation (see p 3). It does this by passing Acts of Parliament. These Acts are then interpreted by the courts, which gives rise to case law. (Note, however, that following a referendum in March 2011, the National Assembly for Wales gained direct law making powers in certain areas without needing the agreement of the UK Parliament – which, historically, has legislated for England and Wales).

SECONDARY (OR DELEGATED) LEGISLATION

Advantanges and disadvangages of delegated legislation

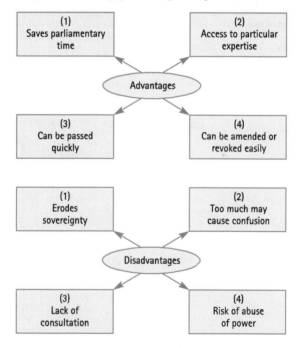

(1) Saves parliamentary time

(2) Access to particular expertise

Advantages

(3) Can be passed quickly

(4) Can be amended or revoked easily

(1) Erodes sovereignty

(2) Too much may cause confusion

Disadvantages

(3) Lack of consultation

(4) Risk of abuse of power

The legisative procedure

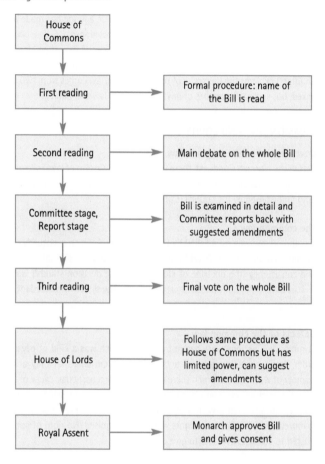

As the name suggests, secondary (or delegated) legislation refers to legislation in the form of rules, directions and orders which are made by other bodies to whom Parliament has delegated its powers. This allows the law to be changed, or set out in more detail, without an Act of Parliament. Statutory Instruments are a very common type of delegated legislation.

CASE LAW

Case law comprises the decisions of the courts. Once a judge has made a decision, it is binding on the parties (although they may appeal it: see Chapters 4 and 5). The legal principle of a case (the *ratio decidendi*) may then, depending on the court, become a legal precedent which other courts have to follow. Chapter 3 explains the hierarchy of the courts. Case law comes from two closely linked, but separate branches of law: the common law and equity.

COMMON LAW AND EQUITY

Development of the common law

Before the Norman Conquest, there was no unified system of law. Following the Norman Conquest, there was a strong centralised government headed by the King and advised by his Council (*Curia Regis*).

The common law

A common law was established by the 'general eyre', which eventually created the first national courts. Good local customs were applied promoting certainty and consistency; the doctrine of *stare decisis* ('the decision stands') was born (see Chapter 3 for a discussion of *stare decisis*). The system of precedent began to emerge.

Defects of the common law

Common law actions were begun by a 'writ', which was a kind of royal court order, setting out the cause of action. The problem was that only a limited number of writs existed, and if there was no writ for a particular cause of action, then the complainant had no legal redress. Hence the expression, 'no writ, no remedy'. In common law, money damages were the only remedy. The law favoured the rich and many rights were not recognised. No right of subpoena existed to compel witnesses to give evidence.

The rise of equity

Dissatisfied parties, unable to gain redress from the common law courts, petitioned the King. These petitions were often passed to the Chancellor (the King's chief minister) for action. Eventually petitions were made directly to the Chancellor and the Court of Chancery began. The Court of Chancery could provide the remedy which best suited the case – 'equity'.

Equity created new rights. New procedures were introduced, for example, the right to subpoena and discovery of documents. Equity also created new remedies, which still exist.

Equitable remedies

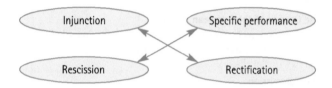

Advantages of equity
Equity was less rigid and formal than the common law, resulting in more flexibility. It was fairer, dealing with cases on their merit. It was described as a 'gloss upon the law', which means that it filled in the gaps in the common law system.

Defects of equity
In its early years, equity lacked certainty. It varied from chancellor to chancellor. It became overburdened and slow moving.

The Judicature Acts 1873–75
The Judicature Acts resolved the difficulties and reorganised the existing courts, fusing the common law courts and the court of chancery. Both common law and equity decisions can now be given in any court. It is important to remember, however, that the two branches of law remain separate. The Judicature Acts also provided that, in the event of a conflict between the rules of the common law and the rules of equity, then equity should prevail. This was retained in the Supreme Court Act 1981 s 49(1).

EUROPEAN UNION LAW

As a result of the European Communities Act 1972, the UK and its citizens are subject to European Union law. European law is now an important source of UK law.

EUROPEAN INSTITUTIONS

The Council of the European Union

This comprises ministers from each member state. The Council of the European Union (also known as the Council of Ministers) is the EU's main legislative body.

The Commission

The Commission has administrative and executive functions. It formulates policies in line with the different Treaties of the European Union. It also has some delegated legislative powers. It manages the EU budget.

The European Parliament

The European Parliament comprises directly elected members from each member state. It is advisory and supervisory. It scrutinises proposals for new laws. In exceptional circumstances, it may veto legislation.

The European Court of Justice

This is made up of a judge from each member state, assisted by Advocates-General. National courts can refer points of Community law to the ECJ for a ruling. It can also hear infringement proceedings against member states which the Commission believes have not upheld Community law.

SOURCES OF COMMUNITY LAW

Primary legislation   Secondary legislation

          +

Community Treaties   *Regulations, Decisions, Directives*

European law has a higher legal status than domestic law. In *Factortame Ltd v Secretary of State for Transport (No. 2)* [1991], the House of Lords considered the relationship between UK and European law. It confirmed that the effect of the European Communities Act 1972 was that European law has supremacy over all UK law (in this case, the Merchant Shipping Act 1988), even in the face of Parliament's express intention to contradict European law. This case has significant constitutional importance, since it suggests that the Parliament of 1972 was able to bind the Parliament of 1988, going against traditional notions of parliamentary sovereignty. Parliament, though, still retains the right to repeal the 1972 Act and, therefore, to leave the jurisdiction of the European Union.

> ### ▶ R v SECRETARY OF STATE FOR TRANSPORT, EX PARTE FACTORTAME (NO. 2) [1991] 1 ALL ER 70
>
> The Merchant Shipping Act 1988 made certain provisions about registration of British fishing vessels: in order to register, the company owning the ship had to be at least 75% owned by British nationals. This then allowed them a valuable share in the UK's fishing quota.
>
> The applicant companies were owned largely by Spanish nationals, who did not qualify. They argued that the MSA 1988 contravened European law. The House of Lords (after a ruling from the ECJ) issued an interim injunction which prevented the government from applying that provision of the Act. This made constitutional history as, in essence, the House of Lords accepted that every statute is intended to comply with European law.

The relationship between domestic law and European law was further explored in *Thoburn v Sunderland City Council* (2003): the so-called 'metric martyrs' case.

> ### ▶ THOBURN v SUNDERLAND CITY COUNCIL [2003] QB 151
>
> The appellant was a greengrocer who appealed against his conviction for using weighing apparatus that did not comply with the Weights and Measures Act 1985 (as amended to comply with European Directive 80/181/EEC). He argued that the Act was inconsistent with section 2(2) of the European Communities Act 1972 and, accordingly, the doctrine of implied repeal operated to overrule the earlier legislation.

Laws LJ rejected this argument and affirmed the position stated in *Factortame* that the obligations created by the European Communities Act 1972 were supreme over national law. He also stated that certain pieces of legislation, such as the European Communities Act 1972 and the Human Rights Act 1998, were constitutional statutes that could not be impliedly repealed.

EUROPEAN CONVENTION ON HUMAN RIGHTS 1950

The Convention for the Protection of Human Rights and Fundamental Freedoms protects the fundamental civil and political rights and freedoms of all members of the signatory States.

Key rights and freedoms of the Convention

Art. 2 Right to life

Art. 3 Prohibition of torture

Art. 4 Prohibition of slavery and forced labour

Art. 5 Right to liberty and security of person

Art. 6 Right to a fair trial

Art. 7 No punishment without law

Art. 8 Right to respect for private and family life

Art. 9 Freedom of thought, conscience, and religion

Art. 10 Right to freedom of expression

Art. 11 Freedom of assembly and association

Art. 12 Right to marry

Art. 14 Prohibition of discrimination

HUMAN RIGHTS ACT 1998

On 2 October 2000, the Human Rights Act 1998 came into force, incorporating the articles of the Convention listed above into UK law. All public bodies have a duty to act in accordance with the Convention (s 6), and individuals who have their rights infringed have a remedy in the domestic courts. Also, the courts must construe all legislation, so far as possible, in a way which is compatible with the Convention (s 3). If it is impossible to do so, a declaration of incompatibility must be made (s 4). However, the courts cannot strike down an Act of Parliament if it does not comply with the Convention.

Section 19 of the Act provides that the Minister in charge of each new Bill must either make a statement of compatibility (that is, say that its provisions are compatible with the Convention) or state that, although such a statement cannot be made, the Government nevertheless wishes Parliament to proceed with the Bill.

An independent Commission to investigate the case for a UK Bill of Rights was launched in March 2011. Its terms of reference are to:

- investigate the creation of a UK Bill of Rights that incorporates and builds on all the obligations under the European Convention on Human Rights.
- examine the operation and implementation of these obligations, and consider ways to promote a better understanding of the true scope of these obligations and liberties.
- provide advice to the Government on the ongoing process to reform the ECHR.

It will consult with the public, judiciary and devolved administrations and legislatures, and aim to report no later than the end of 2012.

You should now be confident that you would be able to tick all of the boxes on the checklist at the beginning of this chapter. To check your knowledge of Sources of law why not visit the companion website and take the Multiple Choice Question test. Check your understanding of the terms and vocabulary used in this chapter with the flashcard glossary.

2

The legal profession

The legal profession in England and Wales is divided into two branches: barristers and solicitors. Each is governed by its own professional body. Solicitors are represented by the Law Society and barristers by the Bar Council.

BARRISTERS: TRAINING AND NATURE OF THE WORK

Barristers are known as the court advocates and consultant specialists of the legal profession.

Barristers' training

Qualifying

| Law degree | Non-law degree |

Common Professional Exam or Graduate Diploma in Law (one year)

Membership of an Inn of Court
(Inner Temple, Middle Temple, Gray's Inn, Lincoln's Inn)

Bar Professional Training Course (BPTC)

Meeting dining requirements

Call to the Bar

Pupillage

Practise as barrister

Continuing Professional Development (CPD)

Nature of the work

Most barristers generally work in chambers, although it is no longer compulsory for them to do so. They are now permitted to practise alone, working from an office or home. The rule that barristers must not deal with clients directly has been modified so that accountants and other professionals can instruct a barrister. Barristers are now allowed to advertise their services in newspapers, a major change introduced under the Courts and Legal Services Act 1990.

Advocates' liability

The House of Lords held in *Arthur JS Hall and Co v Simons* [2002] that it is no longer in the public interest for advocates to have immunity from suit. Barristers can now, therefore, be sued for professional negligence alleged to have occurred in court (barristers could previously be sued only for out-of-court preparatory work).

Conduct of barristers

The conduct of barristers is regulated by the Bar Standards Board, which was established in 2006 as the independent regulatory board of the Bar Council. Its aim is to promote and maintain excellence in the quality of legal services provided by barristers. The Code of Conduct of the Bar of England and Wales sets out the practising requirements, fundamental principles and establishes standards of expected conduct in relation to all aspects of the work of a barrister.

One of the provisions of the Code is the 'cab rank rule' that provides that a barrister must not decline to accept instructions in a case unless to do so would cause him professional embarrassment; if, for example, it concerns an area of law outside of his competence, he is unavailable due to other professional commitments or if he has a connection with the case that would make it difficult for him to maintain his professional independence.

Bar statistics

According to the latest figures (General Council of the Bar, December 2010), there are 12,420 barristers in independent practice in England and Wales, of whom 68% are men. Around seven per cent of all barristers are from an ethnic minority background. Of the 1837 students who commenced the BPTC (then the BVC) in 2007/08, 51% were female and around 20% were from an ethnic minority background.

Queen's Counsel

Senior barristers (and, since the Courts and Legal Services Act 1990, solicitors) can apply to the Lord Chancellor to 'take silk', to become a Queen's Counsel. All barristers who are not QCs ('silks') are known as junior barristers. Around 10% of barristers are QCs. Silks tend to specialise and take on more complex cases than juniors, and can command higher fees.

A new process for the appointment of QCs was developed by the Bar Council and the Law Society and approved by the Lord Chancellor in 2004 and modified in 2006. It aims to ensure that there is a 'fair and transparent means of identifying excellence in advocacy in the higher courts'. The process is based around a set of competencies (competency framework) that barristers are expected to demonstrate, and decisions are made by an independent selection panel. Further details on the process of appointment and the competency framework can be found at www.qcapplications.org.uk.

SOLICITORS: TRAINING AND NATURE OF THE WORK

Nature of the work

The work of a solicitor is very varied. They advise and represent clients, draw up wills, contracts and partnership agreements, do conveyancing, matrimonial work, form companies and deal with accident claims, etc. They are responsible for all the preparatory pre-court work. They are entitled to rights of audience in lower courts and in uncontested cases in the High Court. They can also now gain rights of audience in the higher courts and be appointed QC. The details and implications of this are discussed later in this chapter.

LEGAL EXECUTIVES: ROLE AND TRAINING

The Institute of Legal Executives

The Institute of Legal Executives (ILEX) was established in 1963 and is the governing body for legal executives. The Institute provides training and a career structure for solicitors' staff. Legal executives play an important role and can be involved in specialised areas, such as probate, trust work, conveyancing, matrimonial, civil or criminal litigation. Employed by solicitors, they can deal comprehensively with the client and manage branch offices. Only fellows of ILEX can call themselves Legal Executives.

Solicitors' training

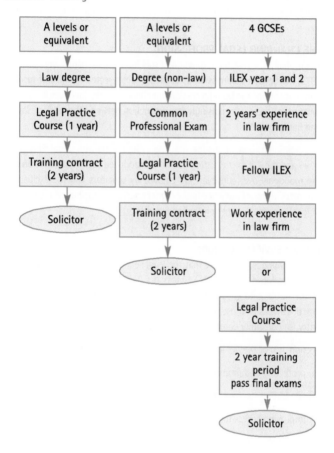

Since the Courts and Legal Services Act (1990) and the Access to Justice Act (1999), legal executives may qualify as advocates.

Training

There is a two part training scheme. Part I involves a broad introduction to key areas of law. In Part II, students study four subjects in more depth. To qualify as a Fellow, a member must have a minimum of five years' experience in legal practice, including a minimum of two years after passing all the examinations.

THE CHANGING LEGAL PROFESSION

Traditionally, the role and regulation of solicitors and barristers were distinct. In 1979, the Benson Commission on Legal Services rejected the idea of fusing the two branches of the legal profession but changes to the law over the years has meant that there is increasingly less distinction between the work of solicitors and barristers.

The Administration of Justice Act 1985, the Courts and Legal Services Act 1990 and the Access to Justice Act 1999 introduced such changes as an end to the monopoly over conveyancing enjoyed by solicitors and the exclusivity of barristers' rights of audience in the higher courts, and facilitated the profession of legal services by other professional bodies.

LEGAL SERVICES ACT 2007

Further changes to the way that the legal services are regulated and delivered were introduced in the Legal Services Act 2007. One of the principal concerns of the Act was to ensure that there were common standards of professional practice across all those offering legal services and to create a common point of entry for consumer complaints about legal services.

Section 1(3) of the Act identified eight regulatory objectives:

(a) protecting and promoting the public interest;

(b) supporting the constitutional principle of the rule of law;

(c) improving access to justice;

(d) protecting and promoting the interests of consumers of legal services;

(e) promoting competition in the provision of legal services;

(f) encouraging an independent, strong, diverse and effective legal profession;

(g) increasing public understanding of the citizen's legal rights and duties;

(h) promoting and maintaining adherence to the professional principles.

The professional principles identified in s 1(1)(h) are those which all 'authorised persons' are expected to follow. Section 18 defines an authorised person as someone who has been authorised by a relevant approved regulator (such as the Law Society, Bar Council, Institute of Legal Executives or the Council for Licensed Conveyancers) in respect of a given legal activity or a licensed body in respect of a given legal activity. The professional principles are listed in s 1(3) as follows:

(a) That authorised persons should act with independence and integrity.

(b) That authorised persons should maintain proper standards of work.

(c) That authorised persons should act in the best interests of their clients.

(d) That persons who exercise before any court a right of audience, or conduct litigation in relation to proceedings in any court, by virtue of being authorised persons should comply with their duty to the court to act with independence in the interests of justice.

(e) That the affairs of clients should be kept confidential.

The Legal Services Act 2007 created the Legal Services Board (LSB) as a single supervisory body that oversees the other approved bodies that regulate the legal profession. Regulators such as the Law Society and the Bar Council will still be responsible for the day-to-day regulation of the work of solicitors and barristers but they will do so within the framework of rules established by the LSB. They will also have a duty to promote the regulatory objectives listed in s 1(3) of the Act and can be penalised for a failure to do so.

Section 114 of the Act creates an Office for Legal Complaints (OLC) and ombudsmen scheme whose structure and operation is outlined in Schedule 15. The legal ombudsman set up by the OLC operates as a single body for all consumer complaints about the legal profession. It commenced operation on 6 October 2010. The Legal Services Ombudsman established by the Courts and Legal Services Act 1990 has been abolished as has the office of Legal Services Complaints Commissioner.

Part 5 of the Legal Services Act 2007 allows Alternative Business Structures (ABSs) to provide legal services to the public in England and Wales. This will permit participation by a larger proportion of individual non-lawyers in a firm than currently permitted, as well as allowing external ownership or part ownership of law firms. They are a new form of practice that will allow non-lawyer organisations to provide legal services, and lawyers much greater flexibility in the way they practise. The introduction of ABSs will allow much wider options in how lawyers and non-lawyers can share the management and control of a business which provides reserved legal services to the public. The first ABSs are able to operate from 6 October 2011.

You should now be confident that you would be able to tick all of the boxes on the checklist at the beginning of this chapter. To check your knowledge of The legal profession why not visit the companion website and take the Multiple Choice Question test. Check your understanding of the terms and vocabulary used in this chapter with the flashcard glossary.

3

The judiciary and judicial decision-making

As of 1st April 2010, the composition of the judiciary is as follows:

■ 12 Justices of the Supreme Court (formerly Lords of Appeal in Ordinary, or Law Lords following the implementation of the changes introduced by the Constitutional Reform Act 2005).

■ 5 Heads of Division:

- Lord Chief Justice, currently Lord Judge, who is the most senior judge in England and Wales, taking over the role of Lord Chancellor.
- Master of the Rolls, currently Lord Neuberger of Abbortsbury, who is the head of the Court of Appeal, Civil Division.
- President of the Queen's Bench Division.
- President of the Family Division.
- Chancellor of the High Court.

■ 37 Lord Justices of Appeal in the Ordinary who sit in the Court of Appeal.

■ 108 High Court judges spread across the three divisions of the High Court with 18 judges in the Chancery Division, 72 in the Queen's Bench Division and 18 in the Family Division.

■ 9 Judge Advocates and 5 Deputy Judge Advocates.

■ 680 circuit judges who sit in the crown and county courts.

■ 1233 Recorders.

■ 448 district judges and 640 deputy district judges who deal with the majority of cases in the county courts and 294 district and deputy district judges who hear cases in magistrates' courts that are too long or complicated to be heard by magistrates.

■ 26966 magistrates.

APPOINTMENT AND TENURE

The Act of Settlement 1701 laid down the statutory foundation for the appointment of judges. Judges hold office *quamdiu se bene gesserint* (for as long as they are of good behaviour). This gives judges security of tenure and they can be removed only upon address of both Houses of Parliament. However, no English judge has been removed under this procedure. This security of tenure remains available to the superior judge but is not enjoyed by circuit judges or recorders; they can be removed by the Lord Chancellor for misbehaviour or incapacity.

The Constitutional Reform Act (2005) created a Judicial Appointments Commission (JAC), which will be responsible for selecting candidates to recommend for judicial appointment to the Secretary of State for Constitutional Affairs (who will also hold the title of Lord Chancellor). The commission will also be responsible for raising the diversity of the judiciary. The commission is comprised of 12 commissioners appointed through open competition and 3 nominated by the Judges' Council.

THE INDEPENDENCE OF THE JUDICIARY

Judges must be completely impartial when applying the law and should not allow any political favour or bias to influence their judgment. The idea of the independence of the judiciary from the State is important to the legal system; protection from removal and the doctrine of judicial immunity reinforces this.

Much stress is laid upon the constitutional importance of the independence of judges and accords with Montesquieu's theory of the separation of the powers. To maintain the idea of non-political interference, judges cannot be members of Parliament.

Prior to the Constitutional Reform Act (2005), the Lord Chancellor's position was incongruous, as he was head of the judiciary and a member of the government. The Act reforms the position of Lord Chancellor, transferring many of his judicial functions to the President of the Courts of England and Wales (the first of which will be the serving Lord Chief Justice). The Lord Chancellor will no longer automatically serve as the speaker of the House of Lords.

The Act also enshrines in law a duty on government ministers to uphold judicial independence, barring them from trying to influence judicial decisions through any special access to judges. The Act also created a new independent Supreme Court, which took over the judicial function of the House of Lords. The change took place on 1st October 2009 and the new Supreme Court has its own staff, budget and building as well as its own independent appointments system.

Judicial immunity from civil suit protects superior judges in respect of their activities during the course of judicial office.

The Constitutional Reform Act 2005 introduced the Judicial Executive Board, whose function is to provide leadership, direction and support to the judiciary. It also established a new Judicial Appointments and Conduct Ombudsman, responsible for investigating and making recommendations concerning complaints about the judicial appointments process, and the handling of complaints in respect of judicial conduct.

JUDICIAL OFFICES
See diagram opposite.

Social background of the judiciary
The judiciary is sometimes criticised because its members are usually drawn from a very elite social background, mostly from public schools and Oxford or Cambridge universities. It is suggested that, because of this and their isolation from life within society, they are out of touch with the moral values of the generation they are trying and sentencing. 18.7% of the judiciary are female, and 4.8% of ethnic minority origin.

The Lord Chief Justice is now head of the judiciary in England and Wales (a role formerly held by the Lord Chancellor). He has many roles, the most important of which include representing the views of the judiciary to Parliament and Government and the welfare, training and guidance of the judiciary.

TRAINING OF JUDGES
Judges receive training from the Judicial Studies Board (JSB). The JSB is an independent judicial body. The Lord Chief Justice now has responsibility for the JSB. He exercises this responsibility through the Judicial Executive Board.

MAGISTRATES

Lay justices
Lay justices sit in magistrates' courts, are part time and are unpaid, receiving only expenses. They try the majority of minor criminal offences; approximately 95% of all criminal offences are processed through the magistrates' court. They do not need legal training, but must undertake a programme of practical training to allow them to sit in court. Lay justices are vital to the legal system as

Judicial offices

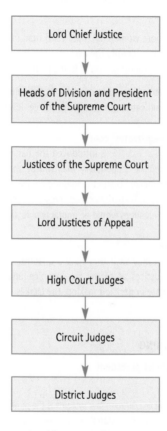

they provide a cheap and quick system of justice. Lay justices are managed by the Ministry of Justice, provisions for organisation are contained in the Courts Act (2003) which introduced significant reforms. They are appointed from individuals put forward by local advisory boards. They must be over 21, not be over 70 and, usually, must live or work in the particular area.

Unlike superior judges, magistrates are not subject to the doctrine of judicial independence; many are local councillors. They must, of course, exercise impartiality on the bench.

The 28,000 magistrates of England and Wales are far more representative of the population they serve.

There are slightly more women (50.6 per cent) than men, and just under eight per cent of magistrates identify themselves as belonging to an ethnic minority – almost exactly the proportion found in the population as a whole.

This is understandable, given that magistrates are volunteers and do not need to achieve legal qualifications or a particular career level.

District judges (magistrates' court)

The Access to Justice Act 1999 introduced the name 'district judge (magistrates' court)' to replace 'stipendiary magistrate', and re-organised all such judges into a single 'bench'. District judges are paid, and are barristers or solicitors with at least 7 years' experience. They preside over busy magistrates' courts where the use of lay justices would be impracticable; they can sit on their own.

The justices' clerk

Lay magistrates can only sit if they have a qualified clerk to assist them. The clerk advises the justices as to the law, practice, and procedure, but is not allowed to participate in decision making. The clerk is salaried, and is usually a barrister or solicitor.

JUDICIAL REASONING

Case law and judicial precedent

Binding decisions

A prominent element of common law systems is the principle of *stare decisis* (literally meaning 'let the decision stand'). It is common to speak today of law being 'judge made'. When deciding a case, judges must look to previous case law decided in similar cases. Judges are bound to decide cases using existing legal principles. The doctrine of judicial precedent depends on the hierarchy of the courts for its operation; courts are bound to follow decisions of higher courts and, usually, previous decisions of their own. Such decisions are described as 'binding' on the lower courts.

Persuasive authorities

The decisions of certain other bodies have persuasive authority only. This means that the courts are not bound to follow them, but that they are very influential and should be taken into account as the court makes its decision. Persuasive authorities include:

- decisions of the Privy Council (often the Privy Council consists of judges who usually sat in the House of Lords or sit in the Supreme Court);

- decisions of the European Court of Human Rights;

- (to a lesser extent) decisions of other jurisdictions, particularly Commonwealth jurisdictions.

Judicial Committee of the House of Lords and the Supreme Court

Significant changes were introduced by Part III of the Constitutional Reform Act 2005 that replaced the House of Lords with a new Supreme Court. Under the old system, the 12 Law Lords not only sat in the House of Lords as the highest appellate court but also, in theory at least, participated in political debate by virtue of their membership of the House of Lords in the sense of its Parliamentary function. The creation of the Supreme Court separated the judicial function from Parliament.

The final cases were heard by the House of Lords on 30 July 2009. Its final judgment was its ruling in the case of Debbie Purdy: her request for a statement of policy from the Director of Public Prosecutions concerning the circumstances in which relatives would be prosecuted for assisting suicide abroad by helping terminally ill individuals travel to organisations such as Dignitas in Switzerland. This was selected as the final case as being one in which the public would have an interest and all 12 Law Lords were present for the final judgment to mark the unique proceedings.

From 1 October 2009, the Supreme Court assumed the appellate jurisdiction of the House of Lords conferred by the Appellate Jurisdiction Acts 1876 and 1888 thus taking over as the final point of appeal for all civil cases in the United Kingdom and all criminal cases in England and Wales and Northern Ireland.

Until 1966, the House of Lords was bound by its own previous decisions (known as the *London Tramways* rule). The 1966 Practice Direction allowed the House of Lords to depart from its own decisions if it appeared 'right to do so'. That said, the House of Lords exercised its power to depart sparingly: it was only used where a previous decision caused injustice, uncertainty or hindered the development of the law, and even then, the House of Lords would consider whether

Hierarchy of English courts

Court	Courts bound by it	Courts it must follow
European Court of Justice	The court which made the preliminary reference	None
Supreme Court	All English courts	None
Court of Appeal	Divisional courts High Court Crown Courts County courts Magistrates' courts	Supreme Court
Divisional courts	High Court Crown Courts County courts Magistrates' courts	Supreme Court Court of Appeal
High Court	County courts Magistrates' courts	Supreme Court Court of Appeal Divisional courts
Crown Courts County courts Magistrates' courts	None	Supreme Court Court of Appeal Divisional courts High Court

legislation was a better alternative to it departing from a previous decision (see *R v Secretary of State for the Home Department, ex parte Khawaja* [1984]).

All decisions of the House of Lords are binding on lower courts. The same rules apply to the decisions of the Supreme Court.

The Court of Appeal (Civil Division)

The Court of Appeal is normally bound by its own previous decisions unless one of the three exceptions from *Young v Bristol Aeroplane* [1944] applies:

■ where two previous Court of Appeal decisions conflict;

■ where a previous decision of the Court of Appeal conflicts with a subsequent decision of the House of Lords/Supreme Court; or

■ where a previous decision of the Court of Appeal was made *per incuriam* (in ignorance of relevant law, or through lack of care).

The Court of Appeal (Criminal Division)

The rules from *Young* above apply, but in addition the court has a discretion to decide that one of its own previous decisions was wrong: *R v Taylor* [1950].

Avoiding precedents

- Distinguishing – a judge finds a significant difference in the material facts of the previous and the present case. The judge can then depart from the law established in the previous case.

- Reversing – a superior court changes the decision of an inferior court in the same case.

- Overruling – a superior court changes the decision of an inferior court in a different case.

Advantages and disadvantages of the traditional operation of judicial precedent

See diagram on p 28.

STATUTORY INTERPRETATION

It is not an easy task for courts to interpret Acts of Parliament. When problems of construction arise, judges have to use their traditional skills to resolve them. There is no Act of Parliament to guide judges in the interpretation of other Acts, although the Interpretation Act 1978 gives some assistance. As more laws become statute based, interpretation of these statutes is a key role of a judge.

Generally, a system of judicial precedent also applies to statutory interpretation: where a higher court has already interpreted the wording of a statute then the lower courts are usually bound by that interpretation. The courts now have an obligation, however, to ensure that their interpretation of statute is compatible with Convention rights. The court may, then, not follow a decision of the higher court if it would mean that to do so would be in breach of a Convention right (see *Fitzpatrick v Sterling Housing Association* [2001] *HL* and *Ghaidan v Mendoza* [2002]).

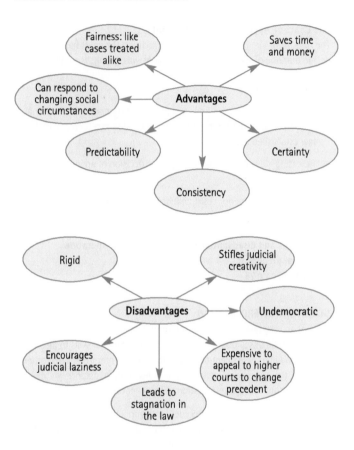

Three main rules

- The **literal rule** provides that simple words that have obvious everyday meanings should be given that meaning by the courts. For example, in *Cutter v Eagle Star Insurance* [1998], the literal rule was used to find that a car park is not a 'road' for the purposes of the Road Traffic Act 1988.

- The **golden rule** provides that words should be given their literal meaning as far as possible unless this would lead to absurdity or an affront to public policy. It is used to prevent undue harshness that would result from the application of the literal rule. For example, in *R v Sigsworth* [1935], the golden rule was used to prevent the defendant from inheriting his mother's property after he murdered her. The Administration of Estates Act 1925 provided that an estate should pass to the issue (children) of a person who died without making a will but the golden rule was used in preference to the literal rule to prevent the absurd situation in which a child who murdered a parent would inherit.

■ The **mischief rule** (or the rule in *Heydon's Case*) provides that the court should look at the law as it existed prior to the enactment of the statute in question to identify the mischief (in the sense of the wrong or the harm) that it sought to remedy. For example, in *Corkery v Carpenter* [1951], it was held that a bicycle was a 'carriage' for the purposes of s 12 of the Licensing Act 1872 which provided for the arrest of a person who was drunk in charge of a carriage on the highway. Although a bicycle does not naturally fall within the meaning of a carriage, the Act was introduced to protect against drunken people using transport on the highway.

Modern approaches

■ The **purposive approach** is based on the mischief rule as it seeks an interpretation of the law that furthers the purpose for which the law was introduced. The House of Lords endorsed this approach to interpretation in *Pepper v Hart* [1993] when it held that the courts could look at *Hansard* (transcripts of Parliamentary debates during the passage of a Bill) to resolve ambiguity by discovering what it was that Parliament intended the words to mean.

■ The **contextual** or **teleological approach** takes into account not just the purpose of the law but also its spirit in the sense of the policy that underpinned the legislation. It is the dominant approach of the European Court of Justice as it favours interpretations of domestic law that promotes the principles of the European Treaties. This leads the domestic courts to depart from the clear words of statutes in favour of an interpretation that upholds the obligations created by European law.

■ Section 3 of the Human Rights Act 1998 provides that 'so far as it is possible to do so, primary legislation and subordinate legislation must be read and given effect in a way that is compatible with Convention rights'. This means that the courts must try to find a way of interpreting domestic legislation in

29

a way that upholds Convention rights. For example, in *R v A* [2001], the defendant argued that the prohibition in s 41 of the Youth Justice and Criminal Evidence Act 1999 on the cross-examination of the victim of rape on her previous sexual history interfered with his right to a fair trial. The House of Lords relied upon s 3(1) to interpret s 41 in such a way that cross-examination would be permitted if it raised a relevant issue that needed to be explored in order for the trial to be fair even though this meant interpreting the statute in a way which, according to Lord Steyn, 'linguistically may appear strained'.

Maxims of interpretation

These offer guidance on how the courts are to interpret the significance of language used.

- *Ejusdem generis* means 'of the same class'. It is used to create a presumption that when a word with a general meaning follows words with more specific meanings, the general word only covers things which are in the same class as the specific words. For example, if a pet-sitting service offered care of 'animals', this could include cows and tigers but if it offered care of 'dogs, cats and other animals', it would be assumed that cows and tigers were excluded because the reference to dogs and cats is taken to mean that the relevant class is domestic pets, not farmyard (cows) or jungle (tiger) animals.

- *Expressio unius est exclusio alterius* means 'the expression of one thing is the exclusion of another'. If a list of words is used, it is assumed that things that are not listed are excluded. For example, in *R v Inhabitants of Sedgley* [1831] a tax imposed on various buildings including coal mines could not be imposed on limestone mines as these were excluded by the specific mention of coal mines.

- *Noscitur a sociis* means that a word can be interpreted by reference to other words with which it is associated. It is assumed that words on a list have something in common with each other so the meaning of any particular word can be inferred from the meaning of the other words on the list. For example, if it is an offence to remove, conceal or dispose of property that could be used to discharge debts when an individual is declared bankrupt, can it be said that a person who fails to mention that he owns 1,000 pairs of shoes has concealed them? This was the issue before the Canadian counts in *R v Goulis* where it was held that as 'remove' and 'dispose' were words that involved positive acts, the meaning to be given to 'conceal' should be narrow so that it covered active steps taken to hide assets rather than the more passive failure to mention them.

Intrinsic aids

The Act itself may offer assistance. Look at:

▪ Title (long or short)

▪ Preamble

▪ Headings

Interpreting European law

The Treaty of Rome (the EC Treaty) confers exclusive jurisdiction on the European Court of Justice (ECJ) to interpret EC law. When a question of European law is raised in the English courts, therefore, the court must make a preliminary reference (under Art 234 of the Treaty) to the ECJ, unless there is a judicial remedy available within UK law (in which case the court may still make a reference if it wishes). Once the answer is received, the English court must then apply it to the case. Lord Bingham in *R v International Stock Exchange ex p Else* [1993] laid down principles relating to when a national court (other than a final appeal court) should make a reference to the ECJ. If:

▪ the facts have been found, and

▪ the issue of European law is critical to the national court's final decision,

then the national court should refer unless that court can, with complete confidence, resolve the issue itself (eg where exactly the same question has been referred before).

You should now be confident that you would be able to tick all of the boxes on the checklist at the beginning of this chapter. To check your knowledge of The judiciary and judicial decision-making why not visit the companion website and take the Multiple Choice Question test. Check your understanding of the terms and vocabulary used in this chapter with the flashcard glossary.

4

The criminal courts and court procedure

CRIMINAL APPEALS STRUCTURE

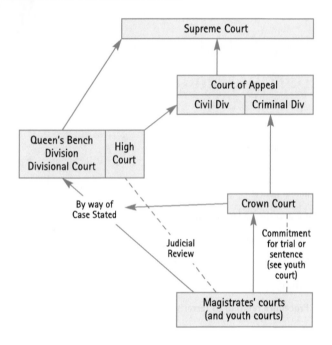

CLASSIFICATION OF OFFENCES (see p 35)

From May 2007, the Ministry of Justice has taken over some of the Home Office's responsibilities for the Criminal Justice system, such as sentencing policy. The MOJ is also responsible for both civil and criminal courts. The Home Office retains many of its existing responsibilities, such as policing and overall crime reduction.

Classification of offences

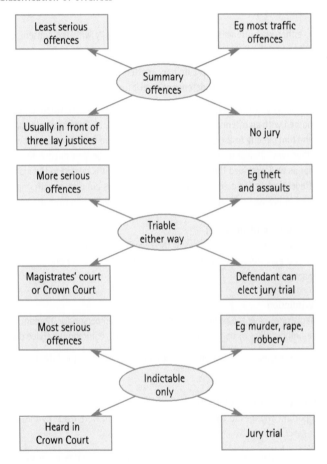

CRIMINAL COURTS

MAGISTRATES' COURTS

With very few exceptions (for example, serious fraud cases), all criminal cases start in the magistrates' court. 95% of cases are dealt with solely by the magistrates' court. Magistrates (also called 'Justices of the Peace') try the following:

- summary offences, tried without a jury; petty motoring offences, common assault, etc;

- either-way offences which are triable summarily with the consent of the accused; theft, burglary, etc;

- magistrates deal with preliminary matters in indictable offences such as legal help and bail. The defendant is sent for trial at the Crown Court.

Section 51 of the Crime and Disorder Act 1998 states that, where an adult is charged with an offence triable only on indictment, the magistrates' court shall send him directly to the Crown Court for trial. Where he is also charged with an either-way offence or a summary offence, he may be sent directly to trial for that as well, provided the magistrates believe that it is related to the indictable offence and, in the case of a summary offence, it is punishable with imprisonment or involves obligatory or discretionary disqualification from driving.

Composition of the court

Between two and seven Justices of the Peace may sit on the bench. Commonly the court is composed of either three Justices of the Peace, or one district judge (magistrates' court).

Jurisdiction

Magistrates have the power to imprison a convicted person for 12 months and can impose fines of up to £5,000, as well as various community service orders.

The sentencing powers of all courts are now governed by the Criminal Justice Act 2003.

Access to Justice Act 1999

Important changes to the magistrates' court system were made by the Access to Justice Act 1999.

The Act contains a range of provisions relating to magistrates and magistrates' courts:

- it provides for various changes to the organisation and management of magistrates' courts;

- it unifies the provincial and metropolitan stipendiary magistrates into a single bench;

■ it removes the requirement for magistrates to sit on cases committed to the Crown Court for sentence and enables the Crown Court, rather than a magistrates' court, to deal with breaches of community sentences imposed by the Crown Court.

The government's objective is to develop a magistrates' court service which is effectively and efficiently managed, at a local level by local people, within a consistent national framework.

Further organisational changes are contained in the Courts Act 2003.

CROWN COURT

Crown Courts try:

■ indictable only offences;

■ either-way offences, where the accused has elected trial by jury.

The court is composed of a judge and a jury. See Chapter 7 for discussion of the jury system.

The Courts Act 1971 introduced the Crown Court. The Crown Court is part of the Supreme Court of Judicature (consisting of the Court of Appeal, the High Court of Justice and the Crown Court). There are three tiers:

■ Queen's Bench Division (QBD) judges trying Class 1 offences (murder, treason, etc);

■ second tier courts may have QBD judges or circuit judges and try Class 2 offences (rape, manslaughter, etc);

■ third tier courts try Class 3 offences, with circuit judges or recorders in charge. Recorders are part time judges appointed on a temporary basis.

Statistics

The Crown Prosecution Service (CPS) was set up in 1986 as the State's official prosecuting agency. In 1999, it underwent fundamental re-organisation and is now based on 42 regional units which correspond to those of the police services of England and Wales.

According to its 2008–09 Annual Report, the CPS provided 532,427 pre-charge decisions, completed 928,708 cases in the magistrates' courts and 103,890 cases in the Crown Court. Of those cases that were prosecuted, 810,605 defend-ants were convicted in the magistrates' courts and 84,000 were convicted in the Crown Court. This represents a reduction in unsuccessful outcomes from 19.4% the previous year to 12.7% in the magistrates' courts and from 24.9% to 19.1% in the Crown Court. The percentage of cases discontinued in the magistrates' courts also fell from 12.7% to 8.7%.

The document *Judicial Statistics 2005* (2005, Department for Constitutional Affairs) notes that, during 2005, just under 67% of the defendants who pleaded not guilty to all counts were acquitted, representing 18% of the total dealt with. Of these, just over 57% were discharged by the judge, 12% were acquitted on the direction of the judge and 31% were acquitted by a jury. After a plea of not guilty to some or all counts, 21% were convicted on a majority verdict by a jury, the remainder being convicted unanimously.

HIGH COURT

This is structured in three divisions:

- Queen's Bench Division;

- Chancery Division; and

- Family Division.

The Access to Justice Act 1999

The Access to Justice Act 1999 establishes the jurisdiction of the High Court to hear cases stated by the Crown Court for an opinion of the High Court. It enables these and certain other applications to the High Court to be listed before a single judge. It provides for the appointment of a Vice President of the Queen's Bench Division. It also prohibits the publication of material likely to identify a child involved in proceedings under the Children Act 1989 before the High Court or a county court; and allows for under 14s to attend criminal trials.

Jurisdiction of single judge of High Court

The Act allows certain applications to be routinely heard by a single judge of the High Court. It does this by removing an obstacle that existed in the previous legislation by which the route of appeal for these cases is to the House of Lords, but the Administration of Justice Act 1960 provided that the House of Lords will only hear appeals in these matters from a Divisional Court (that is, more than one judge) of the High Court. The 1999 Act amends the 1960 Act, so that the House of Lords can hear appeals from a single High Court judge. It allows these cases to be heard by a single judge, while enabling the judge to refer particularly complex cases to a Divisional Court.

The cases in question include:

◻ appeals by way of case stated in criminal causes and matters;

◻ appeals from inferior (civil and criminal) courts and tribunals in contempt of court cases; and

◻ criminal applications for habeas corpus.

Another change made by the 1999 Act concerns appeals from the Crown Court for opinion of the High Court. The Supreme Court Act 1981 gives the High Court specific powers of disposal over appeals by way of case stated coming from a magistrates' court. However, it does not do the same for cases coming from the Crown Court. The Access to Justice Act 1999 provides a statutory footing for the powers of the High Court to deal with appeals by way of case stated coming from the Crown Court.

Judicial review

Where a party in magistrates' court proceedings wishes to complain of illegality, irrationality or procedural impropriety, an application for judicial review can be made. This course of action may be appropriate where it is the decision-making process that is at fault, rather than the actual decision. For consideration of the relationship between judicial review and appeals to the Crown Court, see *R v Hereford Magistrates' Court ex p Rowlands* [1997].

The Administrative Court has a discretionary power to grant three types of order: mandatory orders, quashing orders and prohibiting orders (formerly *mandamus, certiorari* and *prohibition*). The most common remedy sought in appeals from the magistrates' courts is a quashing order. This will be granted in three situations:

◻ where there is an error 'on the face of the record';

◻ where the court has acted in excess of jurisdiction;

◻ where the court has acted in breach of the rules of natural justice.

If granted, the decision of the magistrates will be quashed, and the court will usually direct that the case should be sent back to be heard by a differently constituted bench.

COURT OF APPEAL

Appeals from the Crown Court regarding criminal cases are sent to the Criminal Division of the Court of Appeal. The court hears appeals by the accused on questions of fact, questions of law, the sentence passed on the defendant and appeals by the prosecution on points of law (where an accused has been acquitted). The Criminal Appeal Act 1995 now states that an appeal from the Crown Court against conviction must have leave from the Court of Appeal. The Court of Appeal must allow an appeal against conviction if it feels that the conviction is unsafe and in all other cases it dismisses the appeal.

A conviction may be unsafe even if the applicant has pleaded guilty if:

- the plea was equivocal or mistaken or
- an incorrect ruling of law on admitted facts left the accused with no legal means of avoiding a guilty verdict on those facts (*R v Chalkley* [1997]).

A conviction may be unsafe even if the appellant admitted his guilt at trial if an application that there was no case to answer was wrongly refused. A conviction obtained on this basis is an abuse of process (*R v Smith* [1999]).

In *R v Mullen* [2000] the meaning of 'unsafe' in section 2 of the Criminal Appeal Act 1968 (as amended) was broad enough to permit the quashing of a conviction on the sole ground that there was abuse of process prior to trial.

Composition of court

The Lord Chief Justice, Lords Justices of Appeal and *puisne* judges (High Court judges) from the QBD.

SUPREME COURT AS A COURT OF APPEAL

The Judicial Committee of the House of Lords was historically the highest appellate court in England and Wales. However, as a result of concerns that Law Lords who sit in this court were also involved in the process of creating legislation by virtue of their membership of the House of Lords as a second legislative chamber, the Constitutional Reform Act 2005 created a new court – the Supreme Court – which took over the judicial work of the House of Lords.

Composition of court
The Lords of Appeal in the Ordinary, or Law Lords, became Justices of the Supreme Court when the new court was opened in October 2009.

Types of case
The Supreme Court hears criminal appeals from the Court of Appeal (Criminal Division) or from the Divisional Court of the Queen's Bench Division if leave to appeal has been granted by the lower court or by the Supreme Court itself.

THE YOUTH COURT
The youth court deals with offenders aged between 10 and 17 (Criminal Justice Act 1991), who must be considered in the context of the Children Act 1989. The Children Act 1989 gave statutory recognition to the need to avoid prosecution. Local authorities are required to take reasonable steps to reduce the need to bring criminal proceedings against children and young persons. The Criminal Justice Act 1991 identifies a number of changes, all in line with the welfare principle embodied in the Children Act:

- s 70 renames the juvenile court the 'youth court';

- s 68 extends the jurisdiction so that the youth court and not the magistrates' court will deal with people under 18;

- Pt III gives youth court magistrates new sentencing powers, together with a new scheme of post custody supervision;

- Pt I of the Act applies to offenders of all ages;

- the criteria for passing a custodial sentence are similar to those governing the use of custody for offenders under 21 which were contained in s 1(2) of the Criminal Justice Act 1982. These criteria helped reduce custodial sentences on juvenile offenders between 1980 and 1989.

Children under the age of 10 are irrebuttably presumed innocent. However, the courts now have limited power to grant orders which affect under 10s. The new orders are the *local child curfew* and the *child safety order.*

Section 34 of the Crime and Disorder Act 1998 brought 10–14 year olds within the criminal law by abolishing the rebuttable presumption of *doli incapax* for that age range. Now, prosecutions against 10–14 year olds will no longer have to prove that a defendant knew the difference between right and wrong before proceeding to prove the charge in issue.

The Act also abolished the system of cautioning in respect of young offenders who could be arrested but are not. A new 'final warning scheme' came into effect on 1 June 2000. As part of the new system, the Youth Justice and Criminal Evidence Act 1999 introduced a new sentencing power for magistrates in the youth court dealing with first-time offenders. They can now make a *referral order*, sending the juvenile to a *youth offender panel*.

The range of sentences available to the youth courts differs significantly from those available in the adult magistrates' court. There has been a trend in recent years towards toughening sentences for children and young people. Since April 1999, the courts have been able to make detention and training orders (DTOs). A DTO may be used for 15–17 year olds who are convicted of a serious imprisonable offence. They may also be used for 12–14 year olds if they have a record of persistent offending. The maximum term of any DTO is 24 months. Less severe penalties available to the youth courts include Action Plan Orders, Attendance Centre Orders and Community Punishment Orders. The maximum amount of work which can be imposed in a community service order is 240 hours for offenders aged 16 and 17. Juveniles aged 16 can be compelled to attend an attendance centre for up to 36 hours.

REFORM OF THE CRIMINAL COURTS

Sir Robin Auld conducted a review of the criminal courts in England and Wales, resulting in the 'Review of Criminal Courts' (2001) at the instigation of the Lord Chancellor. Following its publication, the government allowed a period of consultation at the end of which the White Paper *Justice for All* was published in July 2002, followed by the Criminal Justice Act 2003.

The main changes include:

- involving the CPS in charging decisions;
- reforming the system for allocating either way cases by
  - allowing magistrates to be aware of a defendant's previous convictions but retaining the defendant's right to elect trial by jury, and
  - removing committal for sentence in cases tried summarily;

- increasing magistrates' sentencing powers to 12 months so that fewer cases are sent to the Crown Court;

- allowing for a judge-only trial in the Crown Court in complex fraud trials, or where a trial has previously collapsed because of jury tampering (intimidation or bribery), or where there is a risk of this;

- providing for a prosecution right of appeal against a judicial decision to direct or order an acquittal;

- providing for a retrial in very serious cases despite an earlier acquittal if there is new and compelling evidence of guilt (double jeopardy).

THE INVESTIGATION OF CRIME

The 'criminal justice system' has been the subject of heated parliamentary and academic debate in recent years. The uncovering of many miscarriages of justice in the 1980s and 1990s, and the ever-increasing prison population in the face of rising crime figures has led many people to mistrust the police and the system as a whole. A Royal Commission on Criminal Justice was set up in 1991, one of the most significant results of which was the setting up of the Criminal Cases Review Commission to investigate suspected miscarriages of justice. During the 1990s, however, confidence in the police continued to fall, and it plummeted sharply following the publication of the Macpherson Report in February 1999.

The Macpherson Report

Sir William Macpherson was commissioned to lead a judicial inquiry into the police's failure to investigate properly the racist killing of the black London teenager, Stephen Lawrence. The report is most often quoted for its finding that the Metropolitan Police was infected by 'institutional racism', but it identified numerous fundamental failings of the police. Its main recommendations were:

- that the principle against 'double jeopardy' should be abolished. The report recommended that the Court of Appeal should have the power to permit prosecution after acquittal for the same offence 'where fresh and viable evidence is presented'. The trial of the five suspects in the Lawrence case was stopped because there was insufficient evidence to proceed. The defendants were acquitted, and there is a widespread feeling that the guilty may have got away with a serious and repulsive crime. Now see the Criminal Justice Act 2003 (above); and see *R v Dunlop* [2006] discussed in Chapter 7;

- that a ministerial priority should be established for all police services 'to increase trust and confidence in policing among minority ethnic communities';

- that a Freedom of Information Act should apply to all areas of policing, subject only to a 'substantial harm' test for withholding information;

- that the Race Relations Acts should apply to all police officers;

- that the CPS and the police should take particular care to recognise any evidence of racial motivation in a crime.

Largely as a result of this report, Parliament passed the Race Relations (Amendment) Act 2000, which gives all public authorities a duty to:

(a) seek to eliminate unlawful discrimination; and

(b) promote equality of opportunity.

In 2002, Parliament passed the Police Reform Act, which increases the powers of central government over the police, including:

- an annual policy plan is produced by the Home Secretary, setting general policing priorities.

PACE CODES OF PRACTICE

STOP AND SEARCH

The police powers regarding search of an individual are contained in the Police and Criminal Evidence Act (PACE) 1984 and the Home Office Codes of Practice.

Under s 1 of PACE, a police officer can stop, detain and search any person that he reasonably suspects may be carrying stolen or prohibited items and seize them. Articles would include offensive weapons, and articles made and adapted for use in connection with an offence, such as burglary, theft, taking of a motor vehicle or obtaining property by deception; and, since the Criminal Justice Act 2003, articles intended to cause criminal damage.

Other statutes containing stop and search provisions include:

- Misuse of Drugs Act 1971;

- Firearms Act 1968;

- Aviation Security Act 1982;

- Crossbows Act 1987;

- Terrorism Act 2000 and 2006.

Section 2 of PACE provides safeguards for the suspect and indicates the extent to which a police officer can search a suspect in a public place. Section 117 allows a police officer to use reasonable force in the exercise of his powers.

Under s 163 of the Road Traffic Act 1988, a police officer has the power to stop any motor vehicle.

Powers under s 60 of the Criminal Justice and Public Order Act (CJPOA) 1994

Section 60 of the CJPOA 1994 created new stop and search powers in anticipation of violence. The powers must be authorised by a senior officer and must be limited to where there is a fear of an outbreak of violence. The authorising officer must reasonably believe that it is 'expedient' to give an authorisation in order to prevent the occurrence of incidents of serious violence. Thus, the authorisation need not be the only way in which such serious incidents may be prevented.

Further amendments to s 60 were made under the Crime and Disorder Act (CDA) 1998. This is mainly to deal with the problem of troublemakers deliberately wearing facial coverings to conceal their identities, especially when the police are using CCTV cameras.

The Code of Practice (A) for the exercise of statutory powers of stop and search

In view of the wide powers vested in the police in the exercise of stop and search, Code A was revised to reflect the new legislation and to clarify how searches under stop and search powers are to be conducted. The revised Code came into effect in 2006 and supersedes the edition of Code A which came into effect in 2003.

Code A emphasises the following:

1.1 Powers to stop and search must be used fairly, responsibly, with respect for people being searched and without unlawful discrimination. . . .

1.2 The intrusion on the liberty of the person stopped or searched must be brief and detention for the purposes of a search must take place at or near the location of the stop.

1.3 If these fundamental principles are not observed the use of powers to stop and search may be drawn into question. Failure to use the powers in the proper manner reduces their effectiveness. Stop and search can play an important role in the detection and prevention of crime, and using the powers fairly makes them more effective.

1.4 The primary purpose of stop and search powers is to enable officers to allay or confirm suspicions about individuals without exercising their power of arrest. Officers may be required to justify the use or authorisation of such powers, in relation both to individual searches and the overall pattern of their activity in this regard, to their supervisory officers or in court. Any misuse of the powers is likely to be harmful to policing and lead to mistrust of the police. Officers must also be able to explain their actions to the member of the public searched. The misuse of these powers can lead to disciplinary action.

1.5 An officer must not search a person, even with his or her consent, where no power to search is applicable. Even where a person is prepared to submit to a search voluntarily, the person must not be searched unless the necessary legal power exists, and the search must be in accordance with the relevant power and the provisions of this Code. The only exception, where an officer does not require a specific power, applies to searches of persons entering sports grounds or other premises carried out with their consent given as a condition of entry.

ARREST

The normal method of arrest is under a warrant issued by a magistrate or higher judicial officer (s 1 of the Magistrates' Courts Act 1980).

Arrest without a warrant ('summary arrest')

Under s 24 of PACE 1984, the police have wide powers to arrest without warrant.

Originally, under s 24 of PACE, a distinction was made between arrestable and non-arrestable offences. Arrestable offences included very serious offences, such as murder. Where a person was suspected of committing a non-arrestable offence, other conditions applied (s 25 PACE).

However, since 1 January 2006, the distinction between arrestable and non-arrestable offences has been removed. Part 3 Schedule 7 of the Serious Organised Crime and Police Act (SOCPA) 2005 revised s 24 of PACE, inserted s 24A, repealed s 25 and reclassified offences as 'criminal offence' and 'indictable offence'.

Section 24(1) now provides that the police officer can arrest without warrant:

(a) anyone who is about to commit an offence;

(b) anyone who is in the act of committing an offence;

(c) anyone whom s/he reasonably suspects is about to commit an offence;

(d) anyone whom s/he reasonably suspects is actually committing an offence.

Arrest by people other than police officers

In certain circumstances, people other than police officers, such as for example, store detectives, need to make an arrest without a warrant.

They may only do so if:

(a) someone is in the act of committing an indictable offence, or

(b) s/he has reasonable grounds for suspecting that someone might be committing an indictable offence.

There are also conditions attached to the power of arrest becoming exercisable, for example, that it is not reasonably practicable that a police officer makes the arrest.

An arrest will be unlawful where the reasons given by the arresting officer point to an offence for which no power of arrest is given (or for which there is only qualified power of arrest) and it is clear that no other reasons were present to the mind of the officer (*Edwards v DPP* [1993]).

Common law arrest for breach of the peace

Under common law, any individual can arrest anyone who is committing a breach of the peace. A constable can arrest anyone who is obstructing him in the execution of his duty and can call upon the general public to assist him, using reasonable force if necessary; there is no need for arrest to be followed by a charge. The person can be released without being able to claim that he has been falsely imprisoned (*Holgate-Mohammed v Duke* [1984]).

ARREST PROCEDURES

When an arrest is made, the arresting officer must make it clear to the individual that he is being arrested and state the reasons for the arrest. If this is not possible, then the person being arrested should be informed as soon as practicable to do so (s 28 of PACE). If these rules are not observed, it could render the arrest unlawful. People detained under the Terrorism Acts are not subject to Code C. Terrorist suspects are subject to a newly introduced PACE Code H. This deals with the detention, treatment and questioning of terrorist suspects in police custody.

- ▪ s 29 of PACE deals with arrests made while the individual is at the police station voluntarily;

- ▪ s 30 embodies the general requirement whereby an individual must be taken as soon as possible to a police station after arrest.

Duties of the Custody Officer

See diagram on p 49.

Helping with inquiries

The police do not have the power to detain an individual in order to assist them with their inquiries. The person must be actually arrested (*Lemsatef* [1977]).

Section 29 of PACE states that a person who attends a police station to assist the police in their inquiries has the right to leave at any time, if not arrested by the police. There is no legal duty on the police to point this fact out to the person. It is obviously in the interests of the police to gather as much information as they can before charging the suspect. The protection of a suspect's rights under PACE does not come into effect until the suspect has been arrested and, therefore, it is in the interests of the arresting officer to delay arrest.

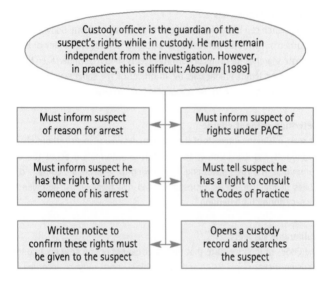

Custody officer is the guardian of the suspect's rights while in custody. He must remain independent from the investigation. However, in practice, this is difficult: *Absolam* [1989]

Must inform suspect of reason for arrest	Must inform suspect of rights under PACE
Must inform suspect he has the right to inform someone of his arrest	Must tell suspect he has a right to consult the Codes of Practice
Written notice to confirm these rights must be given to the suspect	Opens a custody record and searches the suspect

Delay of arrest

Though the police are under no legal duty to inform the suspect of his rights prior to arrest, if it is thought that the delay in arresting the suspect was deliberately to circumvent the protections under PACE, a court may exclude any confession which results from the interview (*Ismail* [1990]).

Booking in

When a police officer detains a suspect, he must be taken as soon as is practicable to a designated police station. Section 36 of PACE provides that the designated station must have a custody officer normally of the rank of sergeant. It is the custody officer who will make the decision whether to detain the suspect.

Searching the suspect

The custody officer searches the suspect and details of the suspect's property are recorded in the custody record. Personal items are usually retained by the suspect (not money or valuables). The custody officer can retain any articles with which he believes the suspect may cause injury to himself or others.

Intimate body searches

A strip search can be carried out if this is necessary. Intimate body searches can be carried out with the permission of an officer at least of the rank of inspector. Intimate searches for drugs or harmful objects should be undertaken by a nurse or doctor or, if not practicable, by an officer of the same sex. Section 117 of PACE allows the police to use reasonable force to search.

Detention without charge

As seen, it is in the interests of the police to detain a suspect without charge for as long as possible in order to gain further information about the offence committed. The rules governing interviewing of suspects are contained in the Codes of Practice. Meals, refreshment and rest breaks must be given to the suspect during his detention.

Vulnerable suspects

The Codes of Practice state that the police cannot obtain answers to questions by using tricks or oppression and vulnerable suspects must be accorded certain rights. The custody officer must arrange for an 'appropriate adult' to attend if the suspect being interviewed is a juvenile, or a person who is mentally disordered or otherwise mentally vulnerable.

The suspect can object to the appropriate adult being present (*DPP v Blake* [1989]). If the suspect is mentally handicapped and makes a confession with no 'appropriate adult' present, the confession may be excluded. If the judge admits the confession, he must give a warning to the jury on the danger of convicting on the basis of the confession (*Lamont* [1989]).

Medical treatment

The custody officer must arrange for medical treatment if a suspect requires it. If a doctor deems a suspect unfit to be interviewed, then a further medical examination should be given before the suspect is interviewed. However, failure to obtain a subsequent medical examination will not breach the Code in itself (*Trussler* [1988]).

Failure to observe these principles may result in any confession being rendered inadmissible in evidence (*Everett* [1988]; *DPP v Blake* [1989]).

Time limits

There are strict time limits on the detention of suspects without charge. Following the Criminal Justice Act 2003 police may detain an arrested person for 36 hours and this can be extended by a further 12 hours by the police to secure or preserve evidence, where the offence is a serious arrestable offence or the offence may lead to serious harm to the security of the State or public order, serious interference with the administration of justice or the investigation of offences, death or injury or substantial financial gain or loss to a person.

If the suspect has been detained for 36 hours, the police must bring him before a magistrates' court to extend the time limit to a maximum of 96 hours. Under the Terrorism Act 2000, different time limits apply.

Review periods

There must be regular review periods of the detention of the suspect. If the suspect has not been charged, the review officer must be at least the rank of inspector and the first review should be carried out no later than six hours from detention; then, every nine hours. If the suspect is charged, the custody officer has the responsibility of review.

Delay in exercising suspect's rights

If a suspect is detained in the police station, he has the right to have a friend or relative informed of his arrest. An officer of the rank of superintendent (or acting rank) (*Alladice* [1988]) can delay the exercise of these rights under s 56(1) of PACE in the following circumstances.

See diagram on p 52.

Grounds for delay

- It is not sufficient ground for delay that an accomplice of the suspect was still at large and might be alerted in a situation where the arrest was made in a public place in front of people known to the suspect (*Alladice* [1988]).

- It was not sufficient ground for delay when the suspect's mother had been informed of the arrest by telephone before the decision to delay access to a solicitor had been made (*Samuel* [1988]).

■ The police cannot delay access to a solicitor on the ground that access may prejudice police inquiries. Access to a solicitor (s 58 of PACE) is a fundamental safeguard under the Act.

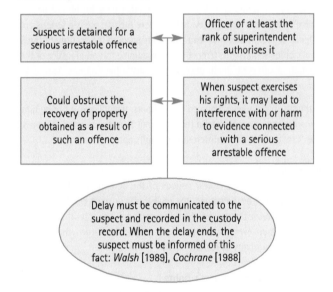

Suspect is detained for a serious arrestable offence

Officer of at least the rank of superintendent authorises it

Could obstruct the recovery of property obtained as a result of such an offence

When suspect exercises his rights, it may lead to interference with or harm to evidence connected with a serious arrestable offence

Delay must be communicated to the suspect and recorded in the custody record. When the delay ends, the suspect must be informed of this fact: *Walsh* [1989], *Cochrane* [1988]

LEGAL ADVICE AT THE POLICE STATION

In *Samuel* [1988], Hodgson LJ commented that the right of access to a solicitor for suspects in police custody is 'one of the most important and fundamental rights of a citizen'.

Section 58(1) of PACE provides that:

> A person arrested and held in custody ... shall be entitled, if he so requests, to consult a solicitor privately at any time.

A suspect is entitled to consult the duty solicitor if he so wishes. However, the role of the lawyer in the police station has been the subject of much debate. Recent research for the Royal Commission on Criminal Justice by Professor John Baldwin, *The Role of Legal Representatives at Police Stations* (1993), concludes that, on the whole, solicitors are performing badly at police interviews. They tend to adopt a passive role, rather than confronting issues on behalf of their client.

Duty solicitor scheme

The current duty solicitor arrangements came into force in April 1990. Important changes centred on the duties of the solicitor in responding to a call:

- previously, a duty solicitor on a rota basis had to accept a call from the regional telephone service. Whether he would attend personally at the police station was at his discretion;

- the new arrangements state that a duty solicitor on a rota, or a panel duty solicitor who accepts a call, must provide initial advice to suspects who have asked for the duty solicitor, by talking to them directly on the telephone. The only circumstances where initial telephone advice does not have to be given are:

  - where the solicitor is already at or near to the police station and can provide advice to the suspect immediately; or
  - the suspect is not capable of speaking to the solicitor because of intoxication or violent behaviour; in these cases, the solicitor must arrange to provide the initial advice as soon as is practicable.

When the initial advice is provided, the solicitor must attend the suspect at the police station:

- if suspect requests this;

- if police intend to hold an identification parade;

- if suspect has been arrested for an offence under s 24 of PACE 1984 and the police wish to question him;

- if suspect complains of serious maltreatment by the police.

ENTRY, SEARCH AND SEIZURE

Section 8 of PACE provides for a general power for magistrates to issue search warrants to the police where there are reasonable grounds for believing that an 'indictable offence' has been committed. The police must have reasonable grounds to suspect that admissible evidence in connection with the offence will be found on the premises and that:

- it is not reasonably practicable to contact any person who could give permission to enter the premises;

■ such a person has unreasonably refused to allow the police to enter the premises or hand over the evidence; or

■ evidence would be hidden, removed or destroyed if the police sought access without a warrant.

Following the changes to PACE made by SOCPA 2005, two different kinds of warrant are now available. One is a traditional search warrant, for specific premises; the other is a warrant covering all premises owned or occupied by a specified person.

Certain articles, such as articles which are subject to legal privilege (that is, between a client and his solicitor), cannot be seized under a warrant. Excluded material includes personal records, such as medical records, specimens for medical purposes and certain journalistic material held in confidence.

In *Central Criminal Court ex p AJD Holdings* [1992], the court stressed that, when police officers request a warrant, they should be clear what evidence it is hoped a search will reveal; further, the application should make it clear how the material relates to the crime which is under investigation.

A search under a warrant 'may only be a search to the extent required for the purpose of which the warrant was issued' (s 16(8) of PACE 1984). In *Chief Constable of the Warwickshire Constabulary ex p Fitzpatrick* [1998], the Divisional Court disapproved of the police practice of using a warrant phrased in broad terms to seize every possible item that could broadly fall within those terms. They should ensure both that the material seized falls within the terms of the warrant and, because such a warrant is granted to search for material of evidential value, that there are reasonable grounds for believing the material has that value and is likely to be of substantial value in the investigation. In this case, in relation to one of the warrants, the police officers went on a 'fishing expedition' and seized a large selection of documents not, on their face, related to the offence under investigation. In doing so, they exceeded the ambit of the warrant (see new changes made by SOCPA 2005).

Entry and search without a warrant

Section 18 of PACE 1984 provides the police with the power to enter and search. These provisions relate to entry and search after the arrest for an arrestable offence of a person who occupies or controls the premises, so that further evidence connected with the offence may be obtained. Section 32 allows the police to enter and search any premises if a suspect is arrested away from the police station and was at the premises on or prior to the arrest, in order to search for evidence of the offence committed.

Where evidence of entry and search after arrest is admitted, it is a question for the jury, not the judge, whether the actual purpose of the police officer's search was to search for such evidence. In *Beckford* [1991], confirmation was given by the Court of Appeal that, under s 32, the police can enter and search premises if the defendant had been in those premises shortly before arrest. The officer's credibility in respect of the search could be tested by the reasons given for the search.

TERRORISM ACT 2000

The Terrorism Act 2000 replaced the 'temporary' provisions contained in the Prevention of Terrorism Act 1989. It gives exceptional stop and search powers to the police. An officer of at least the rank of commander or assistant chief constable, who considers it expedient to do so for the prevention of terrorism, may issue an authorisation specifying a particular area or place. While the order is in effect (no more than 28 days), uniformed officers have the power to stop and search any vehicle or person within that area. 'Terrorism' is not very clearly defined, but includes a whole range of acts if they are designed to influence the government or to intimidate a section of the public, and made for the purpose of advancing a political, religious or ideological cause. The Act has caused much concern among civil liberties groups, who fear that it may be used to control all kinds of disaffected groups who would not normally be branded as 'terrorists' by the general public.

This was considered by the European Court of Human Rights in *Gillan and Quinton v UK* (Application no 4158/05) in which it was held that the police stop and search powers under sections 44–47 of the 2000 Act were too wide and not adequately safeguarded by the law against abuse. The ECtHR considered them to be in violation of article 8 of the European Convention on Human Rights, guaranteeing the right to respect for private and family life.

The Terrorism Act 2006 introduces a number of new offences, including acts preparatory to terrorism and terrorist training offences. It also makes various changes to the detention and treatment of terrorist suspects, including:

■ Introducing warrants to enable the police to search any property owned or controlled by a terrorist suspect.

■ Extending terrorism stop and search powers to cover bays and estuaries.

■ Extending police powers to detain suspects after arrest for up to 28 days (though periods of more than two days must be approved by a judicial authority).

■ Improved search powers at ports.

HOME OFFICE REVIEW OF PACE

In May 2007, the Home Office carried out a review of the PACE Codes of Practice which included a public consultation exercise. The results of the review were published in August 2008 and disclosed a high level of support for the existing framework although it was agreed that the content of the Codes should be subject to annual review to ensure that they are able to take account of statutory change and make any alterations that were considered necessary to aid interpretation and understanding of their provisions. For example, Code A of PACE was amended on 1 January 2009 to reduce the recording requirements so that only the ethnicity of a person who is stopped and searched is recorded.

BAIL

The question of bail can arise at the police station and again when the accused appears before the court. Bail is defined as:

> **The release of a person subject to a duty to surrender to custody at a particular time and place.**

Bail can be conditional or unconditional.

Arrest under warrant

If a person has been arrested by warrant, the warrant will usually have provisions included as to whether bail should be granted. The decision is made by the magistrate who issues the warrant.

Arrest not under warrant

If arrest is not under warrant, the police must act in accordance with the provisions contained in PACE.

Under PACE, the custody officer is responsible for deciding whether to continue the detention of a suspect who has not been charged. After being charged, a person must be released unless:

- the police cannot discover the person's name and address or believe that the information given is false;

- the police reasonably believe that detention is necessary for the person's protection or to prevent the person causing harm to someone else or interfering with property; or

- the police reasonably believe that the person will 'jump bail', interfere with witnesses or otherwise obstruct the course of justice.

The Criminal Justice Act 2003 gives the police the power to grant bail at the place of arrest (known as 'Street Bail').

Bail from court
The granting of bail from court is governed by the Bail Act 1976. Section 4 governs the accused's right to bail. Section 4 gives a right to bail in those cases which do not come within Sched 1 of the Bail Act.

The exceptions to bail are classed in two lists:

- the first list will apply if the defendant is charged with an offence which carries a possible custodial sentence;

- the second list applies if the offence is one which does not carry a custodial sentence.

If it is an imprisonable offence, the court does not have to grant bail if it believes that the defendant may:

- Fail to surrender to custody.

- Commit an offence while out on bail.

- Interfere with witnesses or otherwise obstruct the course of justice.

The Criminal Justice and Public Order Act (CJPOA) 1994 restricts the granting of bail if the defendant commits another offence while already out on bail.

The Criminal Justice and Court Services Act 2000 states that the court must take into account drug misuse when considering bail. And from the Criminal Justice Act 2003 there is a presumption against bail where the defendant is charged with an imprisonable offence, or has tested positive for a Class A drug and refuses treatment.

In 2005, electronic tagging for adults became available as a condition for court bail.

Appeal against refusal to grant bail

An accused person can appeal to the High Court against a magistrates' decision not to grant bail. An accused person not granted bail can also appeal to the Crown Court, which can grant bail:

▪ if the magistrates have remanded the defendant in custody after a full bail application has been made;

▪ if the magistrates have committed the defendant to the Crown Court for trial or sentence; or

▪ if the magistrates have convicted the accused and refused him bail pending appeal to the Crown Court.

INSTITUTING PROCEEDINGS

Prosecutions are usually brought by the Crown Prosecution Service, established by s 1 of the Prosecution of Offences Act 1985. The Crown Prosecution Service works independently from the police: *they* take the decision to prosecute, not police officers. Under s 10 of the Act, the Director of Public Prosecutions, the head of the CPS, must publish a Code for Crown Prosecutors, and cases handed to the CPS by the police must be reviewed against the Code to decide:

▪ whether there is enough evidence to provide a realistic prospect of conviction, and if so,

▪ whether a prosecution is needed in the public interest.

Under s 6 of the Prosecution of Offences Act 1985, a private individual can institute a prosecution. The CPS has the power to take over any private prosecution, either to continue with it or to discontinue it if there is not sufficient evidence to justify the continuation of the case or if it is contrary to public interest to allow the case to proceed. Few private prosecutions are initiated but they do have an important role to play in highlighting public concern over particular issues. In April 1995, the parents of murdered teenager Stephen Lawrence initiated a private prosecution against the five men they believed were responsible for their son's death. The prosecution was unsuccessful as there was insufficient evidence to proceed against two of the defendants and the remaining three defendants were acquitted after the trial judge ruled that witness testimony that was at the heart of the prosecution case was inadmissible.

Laying an information

A prosecution can be started by laying an information – either written or oral – or by charging a person with an offence, which is contained in a charge sheet.

You should now be confident that you would be able to tick all of the boxes on the checklist at the beginning of this chapter. To check your knowledge of The criminal courts and court procedure why not visit the companion website and take the Multiple Choice Question test. Check your understanding of the terms and vocabulary used in this chapter with the flashcard glossary.

5

The civil process

PUBLIC LAW v PRIVATE LAW

PUBLIC LAW

This includes criminal law, constitutional and administrative law. Public law is concerned with the interaction between an individual and the State.

PRIVATE LAW

This includes tort, contract and divorce law. Private law concerns the interaction between legal persons in a community, inasmuch as it does not concern the community as a whole. Here, the term 'legal person' includes both individuals and other bodies having legal personality, such as corporations.

It is possible to be liable in both public and private law.

KEY DIFFERENCES IN CIVIL AND CRIMINAL LAW

Criminal law is concerned with conduct of which the State disapproves and will punish the wrongdoer, seeking to deter others from similar behaviour.

Civil law has a compensatory function. When a dispute arises between two legal persons, rules of civil law are applied to determine which of them is in the right. The party in the wrong must then compensate the other for any loss or damage.

The object of the criminal law is, therefore, punitive; the object of the civil law is to compensate the person wronged.

SEPARATE COURT SYSTEMS

There are separate systems of courts dealing with criminal and civil cases.

COURTS EXERCISING CIVIL JURISDICTION

See facing page for an outline of the courts exercising civil jurisdiction.

Courts exercising civil jurisdiction

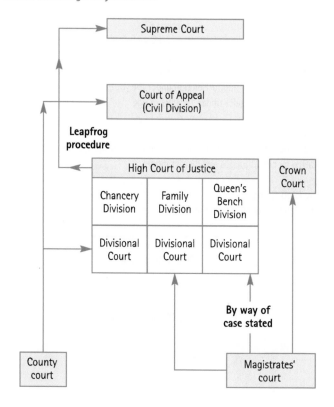

The magistrates' court

Magistrates deal with a large volume of civil cases, in particular with family matters. They deal with issues such as:

- judicial separation;

- maintenance payments;

- affiliation orders;

- guardianship of minors;

- adoption orders;

- case orders.

They also have many administrative tasks, such as issuing and renewing licences, dealing with community charge enforcements and recovery of certain civil debts. The Children Act 1989 has widened the jurisdiction of the magistrates in respect of child law and jurisdiction under the youth court (previously the juvenile court) for juveniles under 17 years of age.

County courts
Established in 1846, county courts provide a cheap system of local justice staffed by circuit judges and district judges.

The High Court
The High Court consists of the following elements.

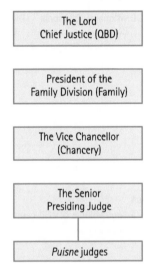

The High Court is split into three basic divisions, each of which is further divided. Any *puisne* judge can deal with any High Court matter, but they tend to specialise.

The Chancery Division

First instance jurisdiction consists of the following elements.

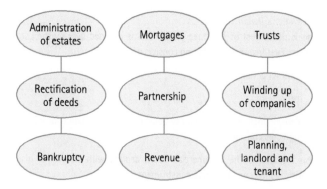

On occasions, other cases are dealt with by other courts, for example:

- the Companies Court;
- the Patents Court;
- the Court of Protection.

The court's appellate jurisdiction hears appeals from decisions of the Inland Revenue Commissioners, and appeals on bankruptcy and land registration cases from the county courts.

The Family Division

First instance jurisdiction (set out in the Supreme Court Act 1981) covers:

- family matters (including all cases concerning marriage – its validity and termination; legitimacy; wardship; adoption; guardianship, custodianship; and family property disputes);

- all issues concerning proceedings under the Children Act 1989; proceedings under the Domestic Violence and Matrimonial Proceedings Act 1976; and s 30 of the Human Fertilisation and Embryology Act 1990.

The court's appellate jurisdiction hears appeals from:

- county courts;

■ magistrates' courts; and

■ Crown Courts.

The Queen's Bench Division

This is the largest of the three divisions. It is presided over by the Lord Chief Justice. First instance jurisdiction consists of:

■ contract actions;

■ tort actions.

The division includes the Admiralty Court dealing with claims for injury or loss through collisions at sea.

Also included is the Commercial Court, dealing with claims for insurance, banking, agency and negotiable instruments.

The appellate jurisdiction of the High Court is as follows:

■ single judge can hear appeals from certain tribunals, and from commercial arbitrators, particularly on points of law;

■ Divisional Court of two judges has a certain civil appeal function, for example, from the Solicitors' Disciplinary Tribunal;

■ also hears appeals from magistrates' court, which have been to the Crown Court for appeal or sentence, by way of a 'case stated' in criminal matters;

■ it oversees the activities of all the inferior courts. Can issue three types of prerogative orders and one prerogative writ: mandatory, quashing and prohibiting orders; and habeas corpus.

The Supreme Court

■ Supreme court of appeal for civil cases in the UK.

■ Appeal to the Supreme Court requires leave of the Court of Appeal or, in certain cases, from the High Court or Divisional Court, for leapfrog appeal under the provisions of the Administration of Justice Act 1960.

■ Appeals to the House are generally only permitted if there is a point of law of general public importance.

■ Appeal committees consist of three Law Lords who report their recommendations to the Appellate Committee.

Judicial Committee of the Privy Council

The Committee hears appeals from Ecclesiastical Courts and certain professional tribunals, and some Commonwealth countries. Members of the Committee consist of:

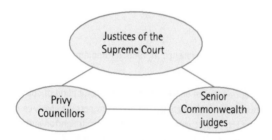

Decisions of the Privy Council are not binding on English and Welsh courts but they do have great persuasive authority.

European Court of Justice

If there is an issue in a case concerning the interpretation of Community law, the court must refer the case to the European Court for a ruling (Art 234 of the EC Treaty).

ORGANISATION OF CIVIL COURTS

There have been many changes in the organisation of civil courts following the recommendations of the Civil Justice Review, initiated in 1985, to speed up the process and improve access to justice.

The Civil Justice Review wanted to meet the public's criticisms that justice was too slow, inaccessible, very expensive, and extremely complex in its process.

Reform of civil litigation

In February 1985, the then Lord Chancellor, Lord Hailsham, began a review into the machinery of civil justice. The review was undertaken by the Lord Chancellor's

Department under the supervision of an advisory committee chaired by Sir Maurice Hodgson. The review centred on five consultative papers concerning civil litigation:

- personal injury;

- small claims;

- Commercial Court;

- debt enforcement;

- housing.

The final report was published in 1988. Its findings were implemented in the Courts and Legal Services Act 1990.

There has been criticism of the controversial redistribution of court business. The Civil Justice Review had concluded that too many personal injury cases were going through the High Court, cases which were in fact straightforward, and there was no need to take up valuable High Court time. Only 36% of awards at trial and 14% of settlements in the High Court were for sums exceeding £20,000. The biggest problem was the delay in the High Court, litigants waiting up to five years or more. The High Court was to be reserved for public law and specialised cases.

Stephen Sedley QC in 'Improving civil justice' (1990) *Civil Justice Quarterly* stated that:

> ... these measures were to allow for a 'judicial fast track' for public law, particularly commercial cases, at the expense of issues arising from things like accidents at work or on the road, wrongful arrests, contracts of employment or tenancies and housing conditions – in other words, individuals' problems.

The Woolf Report: Access to Justice

It was as a result of these concerns that a further review of the civil law process was undertaken by Lord Woolf in 1995. In his Report, Access to Justice (1996), he made around 300 recommendations for the wholesale reform of the civil justice system. Lord Woolf stated that the civil justice system should:

- be *just* in the results it delivers;

- be *fair* in the way it treats litigants;

- offer appropriate procedures at a reasonable *cost*;

- deal with cases with reasonable *speed*;

- be *understandable* to those who use it;

- be *responsive* to the needs of those who use it;

- provide as much *certainty* as the nature of particular cases allows;

- be *effective*: adequately resourced and organised.

He identified the main problems of the old system as cost, delay and complexity:

> These three are interrelated and stem from the uncontrolled nature of the litigation process. In particular, there is no clear judicial responsibility for managing individual cases or for the overall administration of the civil courts.

In the old system that Lord Woolf was examining, the main responsibility for the initiation and conduct of proceedings rested with the parties to each individual case and it was normally the claimant who set the pace. Lord Woolf felt that this was a serious flaw because:

> Without effective judicial control, the adversarial process is likely to encourage an adversarial culture and to degenerate into an environment in which the litigation process is too often seen as a battlefield where no rules apply. In this environment, questions of expense, delay, compromise and fairness have only low priority. The consequence is that the expense is often excessive, disproportionate and unpredictable; and delay is frequently unreasonable.

In order to overcome these problems, Lord Woolf proposed that cases should be managed by the courts and that this should involve control of the timing and cost of cases. He proposed that cases should be allocated to one of three tracks depending on their nature, complexity and value.

These proposals for reform formed the basis of the Civil Procedure Rules which were brought into operation by the Civil Procedure Act 1997 and came into force on 26 April 1999. Since that time, the Civil Procedure Rules have been updated regularly: the 49th update introduced changes in a large number of areas and came into force on 6 April 2009.

THE NEW CIVIL PROCESS

The Civil Procedure Rules (CPR) 1998 apply to both the county court and the High Court. They apply to all cases except (Pt 2) insolvency proceedings, family proceedings and non-contentious probate proceedings. The vocabulary will be more user-friendly, so, for example, what used to be called a 'writ' is now a 'claim form' and a *guardian ad litem* is a 'litigator's friend'.

The overriding objective

The overriding objective of the CPR is to enable the court to deal justly with cases. The first rule reads:

> 1.1(1) These rules are a new procedural code with the overriding objective of enabling the court to deal with cases justly.

This objective includes ensuring that the parties are on an equal footing, and saving expense. When exercising any discretion given by the CPR, the court must, according to r 1.2, have regard to the overriding objective, and a checklist of factors, including the amount of money involved, the complexity of the issue, the parties' financial positions, how the case can be dealt with expeditiously and by allotting an appropriate share of the court's resources while taking into account the needs of others.

Following the Civil Procedure Act 1997, the changes are effected through the new Civil Procedure Rules 1998. These have been supplemented by new practice directions and pre-action protocols. The principal parts of all of these new rules and guidelines are examined below. Thus, 'r 4.1' refers to r 4.1 of the Civil Procedure Rules.

There are three main aspects to the reforms:

(1) Judicial case management

The judge is a case manager in the new regime. He or she is centre stage for the whole action. Previously, lawyers from either side were permitted to wrangle almost endlessly with each other about who should disclose what information and documents to whom and at what stage. Now, the judge is under an obligation 'actively' to manage cases. This includes:

- encouraging parties to co-operate with each other;

- identifying issues in the dispute at an early stage;

- disposing of summary issues which do not need full investigation;

- helping the parties to settle the whole or part of the case;

- fixing timetables for the case hearing and controlling the progress of the case; and

- considering whether the benefits of a particular way of hearing the dispute justify its costs.

If the parties refuse to comply with the rules, the practice directions or the protocols, the judge can exercise disciplinary powers. These include:

- using 'Orders for Costs' against parties (that is, refusing to allow the lawyers who have violated the rules to recover their costs from their client or the other side of the dispute);

- 'unless' orders;

- striking-out;

- refusal to grant extensions of time; and

- refusal to allow documents not previously disclosed to the court and the other side to be relied upon.

One of the greatest changes, however, concerns the spirit of the law. The new style of procedure which is intended to be brisk will be of paramount importance. The courts will become allergic to delay or any of the old, ponderous, long-winded techniques previously used by many lawyers.

(2) Pre-action protocols

Part of the problem in the past has arisen from the fact that the courts can only start to exercise control over the progress of a case, and the way it is handled, once proceedings have been issued. Before that stage, lawyers were at liberty to take inordinate time to do things related to the case, to write to lawyers on the other side of the dispute and so forth. Now, a mechanism allows new pre-action requirements to be enforced. There are now a number of pre-action protocols, including: clinical negligence (including actions against doctors, nurses, dentists, hospitals, health authorities, etc), and personal injury (road accidents, work accidents, etc).

The objects of the protocols are:

- to encourage greater contact between the parties at the earliest opportunity;

- to encourage a better exchange of information;

- to encourage better pre-action investigation;

- to put parties in a position to settle cases fairly and early; and

- to reduce the need for the case going all the way to court.

(3) Alternatives to going to court

Rule 1.4(1) requires the court as a part of its 'active case management' to encourage and facilitate the use of alternative dispute resolution (ADR: see Chapter 6), and r 26.4 allows the court to stay proceedings (that is, halt them) to allow the parties to go to ADR either where the parties themselves request it or where the court 'of its own initiative' considers it appropriate.

At the heart of the new system is the allocation of cases to a 'track' according to their complexity and value.

The small claims track

There is no longer any 'automatic reference' to the small claims track. Claims are allocated to this track in exactly the same way as to the fast or multi-tracks. The concept of an *arbitration*, therefore, disappears and is replaced by a *small claims hearing*. Aspects of the old small claims procedure which are retained include their informality, the interventionist approach adopted by the judiciary, the limited costs regime and the limited grounds for appeal (misconduct of the district judge or an error of law made by the court).

Changes to the handling of small claims are:

- *jurisdiction of up to £5,000* (with the exception of claims for personal injury where the damages sought must be no more than £1,000 and for housing disrepair where the claim for repairs and other work and any other claim for damages are both under £1,000);

- *paper adjudication, if parties consent* – where a judge thinks that paper adjudication may be appropriate, parties will be asked to say whether or not they have any objections within a given time period. If a party does object, the matter will be given a hearing in the normal way;

- *parties need not attend the hearing* – a party not wishing to attend a hearing will be able to give the court and the other party, or parties, written notice that they will not be attending. The notice must be filed with the court seven days before the start of the hearing. This will guarantee that the court will take into account any written evidence that party has sent to the court. A consequence of this is that the judge must give reasons for the decision reached which will be included in the judgment;

- *the introduction of tailored directions* – to be given for some of the most common small claims, for example, spoiled holidays, or wedding videos, road traffic accidents, building disputes.

Parties can consent to use the small claims track even if the value of their claim exceeds the normal value for that track, but subject to the court's approval. The limited cost regime will not apply to these claims, but costs will be limited to the costs that might have been awarded if the claim had been dealt with in the fast track. Parties will also be restricted to a maximum one day hearing.

The fast track
In accordance with one of the main principles of the Woolf reforms, the purpose of the fast track is to provide a streamlined procedure for the handling of moderately valued cases – *those with a value of more than £5,000 but less than £25,000* – in a way which will ensure that the costs remain proportionate to the amount in dispute. The features of the procedure which aim to achieve this are:

- standard directions for trial preparation which avoid complex procedures and multiple experts, with minimum case management intervention by the court;

- a limited period between directions and the start of the trial, or trial period, of around 30 weeks;

- a maximum of one day (five hours) for trial;

- trial period must not exceed three weeks and parties must be given 21 days' notice of the date fixed for trial;

- normally, no oral expert evidence to be given at trial; and fixed costs allowed for the trial which vary depending on the level of advocate.

Directions given to the parties by the judge will normally include a date by which parties must file a listing questionnaire. As with allocation questionnaires, the procedural judge may impose a sanction where a listing questionnaire is not returned by the due date. Listing questionnaires will include information about witnesses, confirm the time needed for trial, parties' availability and the level of advocate for the trial.

The multi-track

The multi-track is intended to provide a flexible regime for the handling of the higher value, more complex claims; that is, those with a *value of over £25,000.*

This track does not provide any standard procedure, such as those for small claims or claims in the fast track. Instead, it offers a range of case management tools – *standard directions, case management conferences and pre-trial reviews* – which can be used in a 'mix and match' way to suit the needs of individual cases. Whichever of these is used to manage the case, the principle of setting a date for trial, or a trial period at the earliest possible time, no matter that it is some way away, will remain paramount.

Where a trial period is given for a multi-track case, this will be one week. Parties will be told initially that their trial will begin on a day within the given week. The rules and practice direction do not set any time period for giving notice to the parties of the date fixed for trial.

Experts

New rules place a clear duty on the court to ensure that 'expert evidence is restricted to that which is reasonably required to resolve the proceedings'. That is to say, expert evidence is only allowed either by way of written report, or orally, where the court gives permission. Equally important is the rules' statement about experts' duties. They state that it is the clear duty of experts to help the *court* on matters within their expertise, bearing in mind that this duty overrides any obligation to the person from whom they have received instructions or by whom they are paid.

There will be greater emphasis in the future on using the opinion of a single expert. Experts are only called to give oral evidence at a trial or hearing if the court gives permission. Experts' written reports must contain a statement that they understand and have complied with their duty to the court. Instructions to experts are no longer privileged and their substance, whether written or oral, must be set out in the expert's report. Thus either side can insist, through the court, on seeing how the other side phrased its request to an expert.

Criticism of the reforms
Professor Michael Zander QC has made substantial criticism of the civil procedure reforms.

At the heart of the Woolf reforms is the mechanism of 'judicial case management'. Looking at the results of an American study about how the system operates in the United States, Zander raises serious questions about whether the Woolf reforms would be subject to similar problems.

The major official study that Zander examined was published by the Institute of Civil Justice at the Rand Corporation in California. The study was based on 10,000 cases in Federal Courts drawn from 16 States. It appears that a range of judicial case management techniques introduced in America had little effect on the time it took to deal with cases, litigation costs and lawyer satisfaction. There was evidence that early judicial case management is associated with significantly increased costs to litigants because lawyer work increases in such circumstances.

The Rand Report explains that case management tends to increase rather than reduce costs because it generates more work by the lawyer. Zander notes that lawyer work may increase as a result of earlier management because lawyers need to respond to a court's management; for example, talking to the litigant and to the other lawyers in advance of a conference with the judge, travelling and spending time at the court house, meeting with the judge and updating the file after conference.

Professor Zander has taken the view that the reasons for delay in civil legal process are not primarily to do with the adversarial nature of civil litigation. The only serious empirical study of the reasons for delay, argues Zander, is that done by KPMG Peat Marwick for the Lord Chancellor's Department in 1994. The KPMG report identified seven causes of delay:

- the nature of the case;

- delay caused by the parties;

- delay caused by their representatives;

- external factors, such as the difficulty of getting experts' reports;

- the judiciary;

- court procedures; and

- court administration.

Defence of the reforms

In 'Further Findings: a Continuing Evaluation of the Civil Justice Reforms' (2002), the Government found that the Woolf reforms were largely successful. The number of claims issued had dropped, claims were settling earlier and the case management conferences were proving useful in more complex cases. The use of single joint experts was also proving effective.

However, the position on costs was less clear. Although the reforms were intended to make litigation less costly, costs had actually appeared to have risen, although it was difficult for the researchers to pinpoint why.

You should now be confident that you would be able to tick all of the boxes on the checklist at the beginning of this chapter. To check your knowledge of The civil process why not visit the companion website and take the Multiple Choice Question test. Check your understanding of the terms and vocabulary used in this chapter with the flashcard glossary.

6

Tribunals, inquiries and alternative dispute resolution

REASONS FOR THEIR CREATION

It is usual to think of legal disputes being settled in the courts but there are other mechanisms for resolution such as the tribunal system and alternative dispute resolution.

ADMINISTRATIVE TRIBUNALS

A substantial number of disputes are dealt with in the network of administrative tribunals that has developed since the development of the Welfare State in the twentieth century with each dealing with a particular area of specialism such as employment, social security and immigration.

Tribunals were seen as a more effective way of dealing with disputes in such specialist areas as they had expertise to deal with the intricacies of the law, and the less formal procedures that they adopted ensured that cases were heard and decided more quickly, an important consideration as cases often involved issues where delay would cause hardship to the individual concerned. Moreover, the lack of formality meant that, in theory at least, there would be less need for legal representation.

The Franks Report

Following concerns that the tribunal system was usurping the role of the courts in adjudicating in disputes between individuals and State bodies, the function of tribunals was subjected to detailed scrutiny by the Franks Committee (1957). The Report of the Franks Committee (Cmnd. 218) listed the strengths of the tribunal system as 'cheapness, accessibility, freedom from technicality, expedition and expert knowledge of their particular subject' but noted that they should be considered as 'part of the machinery of adjudication' rather than as administrative bodies, thus they should be fair, open and impartial. The Franks Report made a number of recommendations for the reform of the tribunal system that would ensure that it achieved these objectives and these were implemented by the Tribunals and Inquiries Act 1958. Further changes were introduced by the Tribunals and Inquiries Act 1992.

The Leggett Report

The tribunal system continued to expand as new tribunals were introduced by legislation to deal with particular disputes. For example, the Mental Health Act 1983 created the Mental Health Review Tribunal with responsibility for hearing applications from people who had been detained under the Act against their wishes. Concerns were raised that there was a lack of consistency as each tribunal was operating under the rules stipulated by the particular piece of legislation that created it. In particular, there were no uniform rules concerning the availability of and procedure for appeals against tribunal decisions.

Sir Andrew Leggett headed a review of the tribunal system which led to the publication of the report 'Tribunals for Users: One System, One Service' (2001). The Leggett Report recommended the unification of the tribunal system into a single administrative body that would deal with around 300,000 cases each year.

TRIBUNALS, COURTS AND ENFORCEMENT ACT 2007

The recommendations of the Leggett Report were enacted by the Tribunals, Courts and Enforcement Act 2007.

The functions of the majority of existing tribunals have been transferred to the new First-tier Tribunal created by s 3 of the Act. This First-tier Tribunal is divided into four Chambers, each of which will have its own area of specialism.

- Social Entitlement Chamber (SEC) covers the following appeals.

  - Decisions made by the Border and Immigration Agency under the Immigration and Asylum Act 1999 concerning whether an applicant and their dependants are destitute and, if so, what support should be provided. This was previously covered by the Asylum Support Tribunal. It does not deal with claims for asylum or other immigration issues.
  - Decisions made by the Criminal Injuries Compensation Authority concerning financial awards to be made to victims of violent crime. This was previously dealt with by the Criminal Injuries Compensation Panel.
  - Decisions about entitlement to a range of welfare benefits such as income support and incapacity benefit as well as dealing with disputes about matters such as child support, statutory sick pay and decisions on council tax benefit.

- Health, Education and Social Care Chamber (HESC) has jurisdiction to hear appeals in the following areas.

  - Decisions from organisations concerned with children and vulnerable adults and those which regulate the provision of social, personal and health care that were previously dealt with by the Care Standards

Tribunal. For example, decisions that a person should be barred from working with children or vulnerable adults or the refusal of registration as a child minder or social worker.

- Applications from individuals detailed under the Mental Health Act 1983 (as amended) which were previously heard by the Mental Health Review Tribunal. For example, the Chamber may order that a detained person is discharged from hospital immediately or is transferred to another hospital.
- Decisions made by Local Education Authorities concerning children with special educational needs. For example, a parent can appeal to HESC if a formal assessment of their child's special educational needs is not carried out. This jurisdiction was previously exercised by the Special Educational Needs and Disability Tribunal.

■ War Pensions and Armed Forces Compensation Chamber (WPAFC) hears appeals from servicemen and ex-servicemen concerning the following.

- Decisions of the Secretary of Defence concerning entitlement and calculation of a War Pension under the War Pensions Act 1919.
- Decisions concerning entitlement and calculation of compensation under the Armed Forces Compensation Scheme in respect of injuries incurred after April 2005.

■ Tax hears appeals from decisions made by Her Majesty's Revenue and Customs concerning direct taxes, such as income tax and corporation tax, and indirect taxes levied on goods and services such as VAT.

It is envisaged that further tribunals will be added to the new structure as part of a phased implementation programme.

The Act also created an Upper Tribunal which, under s 11, provides the normal route of appeal from decisions made by the First-tier Tribunal on a point of law, thus creating a reasonably unified appeal structure. However, some decisions do not carry a right to appeal so decisions relating to asylum support and criminal injuries compensation can be challenged only by judicial review. Some cases commence directly in the Upper Tribunal.

The Upper Tribunal is divided into three Chambers:

■ Administrative Appeals Chamber

■ Finance and Tax Chamber

■ Lands Chamber

According to s 13, a route of appeal lies from decisions of the Upper Chamber to the Court of Appeal on a point of law.

Administrative Justice and Tribunals Council
Section 44 of the Tribunals, Courts and Enforcement Act 2007 creates the Administrative Justice and Tribunals Council: a public body with responsibility for supervising and regulating the administrative justice system. In relation to the new tribunal system, the Council must review and report on the operation of the tribunals under its supervision and scrutinise legislation relating to tribunals.

COURTS WITH SPECIAL JURISDICTION

- Restrictive Practices Court;
- Coroners Court;
- Courts Martial; and
- Ecclesiastical Courts.

INQUIRIES

Inquiries are usually established on an *ad hoc* basis when it is necessary to deal with a specific issue, for example:

- to investigate major accidents by air, sea or rail;
- to investigate companies under the Companies Act 2006; and
- inquiries into a specific event.

Their role is fact-finding.

ALTERNATIVE DISPUTE RESOLUTION

ARBITRATION
Arbitration is a means of settling disputes other than by court action and arises when one or more persons are appointed to hear the arguments put forward by

the parties and to decide upon them. Many contracts today contain arbitration clauses.

Advantages of arbitration

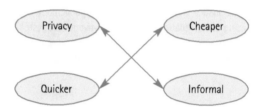

- A matter can be referred to arbitration by the court either by Acts of Parliament or by agreement, if the issues concerned are complex and technical.

- Agreement can be in any form, oral or written, but the Arbitration Act 1996 only applies to agreements in writing.

- The agreement normally names the arbitrator, but the agreement can specify a specific body; for example, a trade or profession.

- The arbitrator can examine witnesses and parties concerned on oath if necessary, and require parties to submit documents, accounts, etc.

- The arbitrator makes an award. This is final and binding on the parties – no rights of appeal; the arbitrator can order the party to pay the entire costs of the proceedings if they lose.

- Where there is an arbitration agreement and one party nevertheless brings court proceedings on the application of the other party, the court will 'stay' proceedings.

- The arbitration agreement must cover the dispute which is before the court, otherwise the court will not stay proceedings.

- The person asking for the stay must have taken no part in the court proceedings.

Procedure in arbitration

Duty of arbitrator

The duty of the arbitrator is to resolve the dispute by making an award. The arbitrator can employ a legal adviser if necessary to help draw up the award if s/he feels s/he is not competent to deal with the legal issues involved. The arbitrator fixes the time and place for hearing the parties and will inform them of this arrangement. If the arbitrator has specialised technical knowledge, s/he can dispense with the need for expert witnesses. This reduces costs.

If an important point of law arises, the arbitrator can 'state a case' for the opinion of the court. When the opinion of the court is given, the arbitrator applies the law to the facts of the case and makes the award. The arbitrator can decide that it is not necessary to 'state a case'. S/he can, however, be compelled to do this by one of the parties.

The award is final. However, the court can set aside an award on procedural grounds if:

- the arbitrator has misconducted her/himself, or the award was obtained by improper means;

- there is a 'serious irregularity' in the conduct of the proceedings or of the award itself;

- the arbitrator refuses to hear one of the parties;

- the witnesses were examined in the absence of one of the parties;

- the arbitrator has been in communication with one of the parties about the issues involved.

(See Arbitration Act 1996, s 68(1).)

Enforcement

The party in whose favour the award has been made can enforce the award as if it were a court judgment.

The Arbitration Act 1996 provides that the object of arbitration is the fair resolution of disputes by an impartial tribunal without unnecessary delay or expense. It says that the parties should be free to agree how their disputes are resolved, subject only to such safeguards as are necessary in the public interest.

Courts can only intervene as far as the Act allows them to do so. In order to be governed by the Act, arbitration agreements must be made in writing. Under the Act, a party is entitled to appeal to a law court to challenge the award made in arbitral proceedings on the ground of a 'serious irregularity' affecting the tribunal, the proceedings or the award. Nonetheless, the Act greatly restricts the scope of appeals that may be made to a law court on a point of law.

MEDIATION

Mediation is the process whereby a third party acts as the medium through which two disputing parties can communicate and negotiate in order to resolve a problem without recourse to the courts. It is most commonly used in divorce matters. Mediation was particularly emphasised in the Family Law Act 1996. However, Lord Irvine (then Lord Chancellor) announced in 1999 that the proposals in the 1996 Act would not be implemented in 2000 as intended, because of the extent of the criticism from legal practitioners and academics. This did not signal the end of mediation altogether, but its scope is undoubtedly narrower than Parliament had intended in 1996. It remains government policy to encourage parties to mediate rather than go to court.

CONCILIATION

Similar to mediation, but the conciliator takes a more interventionist approach, suggesting possible solutions to aid settlement.

You should now be confident that you would be able to tick all of the boxes on the checklist at the beginning of this chapter. To check your knowledge of Tribunals, inquiries and alternative dispute resolution why not visit the companion website and take the Multiple Choice Question test. Check your understanding of the terms and vocabulary used in this chapter with the flashcard glossary.

The jury system

7

COMPOSITION OF JURIES

Juries are used mainly in criminal proceedings. They are used in trials for indictable offences, and (usually) when an adult is charged with a triable either way offence, he can elect to be tried by jury. A jury is only rarely used in civil proceedings. The Administration of Justice Act 1933 limited its use to cases such as libel and fraud.

The jury consists of twelve men and women between 18 and 70 who meet certain eligibility requirements. In an attempt to improve diversity in juries, the Criminal Justice Act 2003 provided that no-one could be excused from jury service simply because of their job. Now lawyers and even judges may be called up for jury service.

CHALLENGING JURY MEMBERSHIP

Under very limited circumstances, jury membership can be challenged by either side.

Jury membership may be challenged for cause if:

- the juror is in fact not qualified (see CJA 2003 s 321 and Schedule 33 for details (amending the Juries Act));

- the juror is biased; or

- the juror may be reasonably suspected of bias against the defendant (s 12(4)).

Juries Act 1974

The prosecution has a right to challenge as well as the defence, and also has the right to ask a juror to 'stand by' for the Crown.

The Attorney General has laid down guidelines as to when the prosecution can exercise the right:

- if a jury check shows information to support exercising the right to stand by; or

- if the person to be sworn in as a juror is unsuitable and the defence agree (Practice Note (1988)).

Challenging jury membership

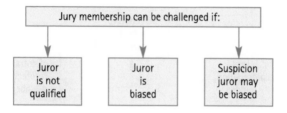

Either side can challenge the array.

Peremptory challenge
In the past, the defence had the right of peremptory challenge, whereby it could challenge up to three jurors without giving any reasons. The right to peremptory challenge was abolished by the Criminal Justice Act 1988 (s 118).

JURY VETTING
The panel is selected at random, and any party to the proceedings can inspect the panel from which the jurors will be chosen.

Jury vetting is the investigation of jurors' backgrounds to determine whether they are suitable for jury service.

The practice first came to public notice in 1978 during the 'ABC trial', a case brought under the Official Secrets Act 1911.

Lord Denning challenged the practice of jury 'settling': *Crown Court at Sheffield ex p Brownlow* [1980]. However, *R v Mason* [1981] established that the practice is not unlawful.

The constitutional position of this practice is much in doubt and has been criticised. However, the legitimacy and that of the Crown's right to 'stand by' potential jurors is clearly stated by the Court of Appeal in *R v Bettaney* [1985]. The Attorney General issued a Practice Note in 1988 and also issued a statement confirming the previous guidelines.

See diagram on p 88.

Arguments for and against the jury system

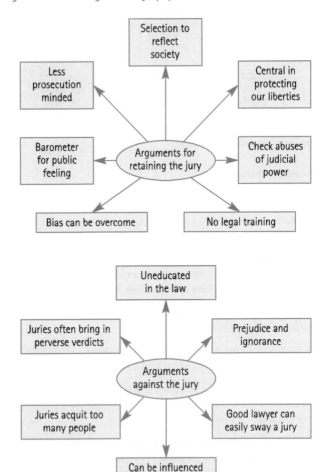

THE ROLE OF THE JURY

To decide the facts of the case

↓

They are lay persons, they have no knowledge of law and are not competent to put forward any opinion on law. They rely on their common sense to assess the accused and the evidence against him in order to reach a verdict. If the verdict is an acquittal, it is almost always unchallengeable.

Function of the judge

↓

Inter alia, to explain the law to the jury so it can reach a verdict. At the conclusion of the evidence, to sum up the case before the jury retires to reach a verdict. The judge has no judicial power to instruct a jury to convict an accused: *DPP v Stonehouse* [1978].

▪ Once the accused is acquitted, he generally cannot be charged with the same offence again. This has been much criticised, most recently in the Macpherson Report (1999). The Criminal Justice Act 2003 abolished the rule against double jeopardy in serious cases where there is new and compelling evidence of guilt. The first case to be decided since the double jeopardy rule was abolished was *R v Dunlop* [2006] EWCA Crim 1354.

▶ R v DUNLOP [2006] EWCA 1354

The Defendant had been charged with the murder of his girlfriend, Julie Hogg. In May 1991, the jury had failed to reach a verdict. In October 1991, he was acquitted of the offence by another jury. In 2006, following a confession made earlier to the police, which constituted 'new and compelling evidence' under Part 10 of the Criminal Justice Act 2003, the Defendant was retried and convicted of Ms Hogg's murder. This is a very current topic for exam questions.

- Section 36 of the Criminal Justice Act 1972 does provide for a procedure whereby points of law which arise in a criminal case where the defendant has been acquitted can be referred to the Court of Appeal by the Attorney General to see if any loopholes in the law can be amended. This does not, however, affect the original verdict.

- Under s 54 of the Criminal Procedure and Investigations Act 1996, the prosecution can appeal to the High Court to quash a defendant's acquittal and order a retrial in the Crown Court where the acquittal was as a result of jury tampering.

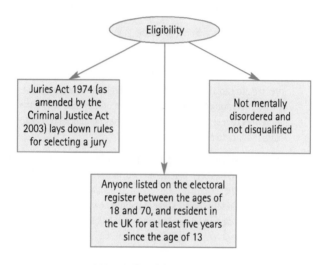

CHANGES TO THE JURY SYSTEM

The jury is thought to be one of the most vital features of the English legal system and a fundamental safeguard to our liberty. However, the jury has been criticised over the years.

The most influential of the recent studies is Penny Darbyshire's 'The lamp that shows that freedom lives – is it worth a candle?', which was produced as a result of her experience of serving on a jury. Her aim was:

... to question the traditional qualifications used in praise and defence of the jury, suggesting that some of them are conceptually unsound ... [to] argue that jury defenders inflate the jury's importance by portraying the 'right' to jury trial as central to the criminal justice system and as a guardian of due process and civil liberties.

Darbyshire criticises the traditional view of the jury and criticises those commentators who emphasise the 'mystery' of the jury. Juries, she states, are not a representative sample of the population. She points out that they are:

An antidemocratic, irrational and haphazard legislator, whose erratic and secret decisions run counter to the rule of the law.

The Royal Commission on Criminal Justice has put forward proposals to reduce the role of the jury in criminal trials, and the Criminal Justice Act 2003 contains provisions for judge-only trials in the Crown Court (see Chapter 4).

Although the jury is seen to be an important cornerstone of the English legal system, few in-depth studies have been made of it. Some commentators have tended to view the jury in a romantic light, which, it is argued, is detrimental to change in the justice system.

Darbyshire's arguments tend to imply that because it plays such a small role in the minority of cases, its passing would not be cause for lament.

Others argue, however, that the jury system performs a very important service and it should be protected at all costs.

TRIAL WITHOUT A JURY

The most prominent issue at present concerns the abolition of the right to a jury trial in certain cases. In 1986, the Roskill Report advocated the abolition of the right to jury trial in complex fraud cases as did the Auld Committee in 2001. These proposals were adopted by the government in s 43 of the Criminal Justice Act 2003 which gave prosecutors the power to apply for serious and/or complex fraud trials to be conducted without a jury. Permission would be granted if:

The complexity of the trial or the length of the trial (or both) is likely to make the trial so burdensome to the members of a jury hearing the trial that the interests of justice require that serious consideration should be given to the question of whether the trial should be conducted without a jury (s 43(5) Criminal Justice Act 2003).

Due to the controversial nature of this provision, it could not be implemented without an affirmative resolution in the House of Commons and the House of Lords (Criminal Justice Act 2003 (s 330(5)(b)). Despite the government's commitment to the introduction of section 43, there was lack of support for its introduction, especially in the House of Lords, so the government sought to achieve the abolition of the right to jury trial in complex fraud cases by introducing specific legislation in the form of the Fraud (Trials without a Jury) Bill 2006. A detailed outline of the government's arguments in favour of the Bill can be found in the Fraud (Trial without a Jury) Bill Research Paper (06/57). The Bill did not find support in the House of Lords and did not proceed.

If the Protection of Freedoms Bill (2011) is enacted, it will cause section 43 of the Criminal Justice Act 2003 to be omitted.

A similar provision that curtails the right to jury trial in cases where there is a serious risk of jury tampering did not receive such opposition and came into force on 24 July 2007. Section 44 of the Criminal Justice Act 2003 allows the judge, following an application by the prosecution, to order that a trial should proceed at Crown Court without a jury if two conditions are satisfied.

- There is evidence of real and present danger that jury tampering would take place: s 44(4).
- Notwithstanding any steps (including the provision of police protection) which might reasonably be taken to prevent jury tampering, the likelihood that it would take place would be so substantial as to make it necessary in the interests of justice for the trial to be conducted without a jury: s 44(5).

Section 44(6) gives three examples of situations that might present a real and present danger of jury tampering.

- A retrial of a case in which the jury at the previous trial were discharged due to tampering.
- A case in which tampering has taken place in previous proceedings involving the defendant or any of the defendants.

▨ Cases in which there has been intimidation or attempted intimidation of any person likely to be a witness in the trial.

In cases where the judge makes an order that the case can proceed without a jury, this decision can be appealed to the Court of Appeal in an attempt to restore the defendant's right to trial by jury. On 18 June 2009, the court rejected such an application in *R v T* [2009] EWCA Crim 1035 and ruled that the trial of the four defendants who were charged with an armed robbery at Heathrow Airport in February 2004 would be heard by a judge only.

REFORM OF THE JURY SYSTEM

THE 1999 JURY PROPOSALS

In 1999, the government announced its intention to introduce legislation to curb the right to jury trial. In essence, it wished, in cases triable either way, to disallow a defendant from insisting upon trial by jury in circumstances where magistrates believed that they were well suited to hear the case. More than 18,500 defendants a year would have lost their right to trial by jury under these plans. The plans were advanced by the government, according to its own contentions, to speed up the hearing of criminal cases. The proposed reform was widely condemned by civil rights groups, the Bar and other lawyers.

The government decided to push ahead with the change after finding that many people who opt in the early stages of their cases for trial by jury changed their plea to guilty before the trial was heard. Home Office research showed that more than 70% of those who opt for jury trial plead guilty by the day their Crown Court case opens. The average cost of a jury trial is £13,500, compared with £2,500 for a hearing by magistrates.

In order to research the matter further, and as part of a review of the whole criminal justice system, the government commissioned the Auld Report. It was published in September 2001, and its main recommendations on the jury system were as follows:

▨ Jurors should be more widely representative than they are of the national and local communities from which they are drawn. Except for those with criminal convictions or mental disorder, no one in future should be ineligible for or excusable as of right from jury service. These proposals are now contained in the Criminal Justice Act 2003.

■ In 2007, the Ministry of Justice commissioned a report: 'Diversity and Fairness in the Jury System'. The conclusions of this report were encouraging. It found that women and ethnic minority groups were not under-represented in Crown Courts, and that most jury pools were representative of the local community. It also found that racially-mixed juries did not discriminate against defendants on the grounds of ethnicity.

■ The law should not be extended to permit more intrusive research than is already possible into the workings of juries. The law should be declared, by statute if need be, that juries have no right to acquit defendants in defiance of the law or in disregard of the evidence. None of these proposals have been made law.

■ The defendant should no longer have an elective right to trial by jury in 'either way' cases. Under the Criminal Justice Act 2003, defendants have retained this right, but there are provisions for judge-only trials (see Chapter 4).

You should now be confident that you would be able to tick all of the boxes on the checklist at the beginning of this chapter. To check your knowledge of The jury system why not visit the companion website and take the Multiple Choice Question test. Check your understanding of the terms and vocabulary used in this chapter with the flashcard glossary.

Access to justice

8

The Access to Justice Act 1999 introduced a new structure to help people who cannot otherwise afford to use lawyers to do so. It introduced the Legal Services Commission (LSC) to replace the Legal Aid Board, and the Community Legal Service (CLS) to organise the provision of free legal services locally. The Act also introduces the Criminal Defence Service (CDS) to provide lawyers to people without sufficient means who need defence lawyers in criminal cases.

THE HISTORY OF LEGAL AID

Legal aid was not available until after the Second World War; prior to that, individuals needing legal advice had to depend on the generosity of lawyers taking their case for a bare fee.

The State system of legal aid was created through a series of statutes:

- Legal Aid Acts 1949 and 1964;

- Criminal Justice Act 1967;

- Legal Advice and Assistance Act 1972;

- Legal Aid Act 1974;

- Legal Aid Act 1979 (as amended 1985);

- Legal Aid Act 1988.

Problems with legal aid

By the 1980s, the state funding of legal services had developed into six separate schemes, but costs were rising and the Conservative government reduced eligibility for funding in the 1990s by way of stricter means testing. This led to criticisms that access to justice was being restricted to the very poor and those rich enough to fund themselves. Other problems also existed (see pp 99–100).

Eligibility for legal aid

Eligibility for legal aid is dependent on the individual's financial circumstances.

Legal aid limits were set at the same level as supplementary benefits in 1974 and increased each year as a result. The Murphy Report concluded that, since 1979, more than 10 million people have lost their eligibility for civil legal aid on the basis of income.

The Legal Aid Act 1988

Until 1999, the legal aid scheme and the Legal Aid Board were governed by the Legal Aid Act 1988. This Act has now been repealed, and 'legal aid' in its original form no longer exists.

THE COMMUNITY LEGAL SERVICE

Until recently, about £800 million a year was spent on lawyers' fees under the civil legal aid system. Another £150 million a year from local government, central government, charities and businesses is spent on the voluntary advice sector, including Citizens' Advice Bureaux, law centres and other advice centres. The Legal Services Commission (LSC) (replacing the Legal Aid Board) was intended to take the lead in establishing a Community Legal Service (CLS), co-ordinating the provision of legal services in every region. The LSC manages the CLS fund, which has replaced legal aid in civil and family cases.

In 2004, the Community Legal Service Direct was established. It is a national telephone and website service, offering free legal advice on civil matters as an alternative to face-to-face advice.

THE REASONS FOR CHANGE

The main reasons that the government decided a change was necessary were as follows:

- The system was too heavily biased towards expensive court based solutions to people's problems.

- Despite a merits test, legal aid was sometimes used to fund cases that appear to be undeserving.

- It was not possible to control spending effectively. From 1992–93 to 1997–98, spending on civil and family legal aid grew by 35% from £586 million to £793 million; but, at the same time, the number of cases funded actually fell by 31% from 419,861 to 319,432.

- In the ordinary legal aid system, lawyers were paid according to the amount of work claimed for, so there was no incentive to handle cases quickly or work efficiently.

HOW THE NEW SYSTEM WORKS

The LSC buys services for the public under contracts. Only lawyers and other providers with contracts are able to work under the new scheme. This enables budgets to be strictly controlled, helps to ensure quality of service, and provides a basis for competition between providers. The fund is targeted towards those people who are most in need of help, and high priority cases. There is no absolute entitlement to help, and the fund is not spent on cases which could be financed by other means, such as conditional fee arrangements ('no win, no fee'). Also, those who can afford to contribute towards their legal expenses are required to do so. The government has been encouraging a widening of legal insurance cover and conditional fees for those people who are not eligible for funding.

THE ACCESS TO JUSTICE ACT 1999

Under the new system, legal aid is no longer usually available for:

- those seeking accident compensation (except clinical negligence cases);

- disputes about inheritance under a will or an intestacy;

- matters affecting the administration of a trust or the position of a trustee;

- defamation;

- company or partnership law;

- matters before the Lands Tribunal, or Employment Tribunal;

- cases between landowners over a disputed boundary of adjacent property; and

- cases pursued in the course of a business.

The hope is that the extension of conditional fees in these areas will provide increased public access to lawyers.

Conditional fees

The right to use 'no win, no fee' agreements to pursue civil law claims was extended by the Conditional Fee Agreement Regulations 2000. The order allows lawyers to offer conditional fee agreements to their clients in all civil cases excluding family cases.

With the introduction of companies such as 'Claims Direct' and 'The Accident Group', the last few years have seen a significant increase in the number of people taking advantage of conditional fee arrangements (CFAs) to bring personal injury claims. The government has noted that many of these people would have been unable to afford to pursue their claims at all without conditional fees – people who are only just above the legal aid/CLS limit, and are far from well off.

The Access to Justice Act 1999 reformed the law relating to conditional fees. It enables the court to order the losing party to pay, in addition to the other party's normal legal costs, the uplift on the successful party's lawyers' fees. Also, in any case where a litigant has insured against facing an order for the other side's costs, the losing party may be ordered to cover the premium paid by the successful party for that insurance. See *Callery v Gray* [2002] and *Halloran v Delaney* [2002].

In November 2005, the Conditional Fee Agreements (Revocation) Regulations 2005 revoked the previous CFA regulations, which the legal profession thought were too complicated. The new system gives the Law Society more flexibility when dealing with clients and it is hoped will reduce the high level of satellite litigation that resulted from the old regulations.

Clinical negligence cases

Funding has been retained for clinical negligence cases as it is much more difficult for litigants to secure conditional fee arrangements for these claims than it is in other personal injury claims. It is a very specialist area of litigation, and it can be difficult to identify at the outset whether a case has merit, and even as the case unfolds whether the alleged negligence has caused the ailment or injury. The Lord Chancellor stated in 1999 that lawyers needed time to modernise their firms in such a way as to make them able to take on clinical negligence claims regardless of the means of the claimant. The legal profession has, over the past few years, become more and more specialised, and there are now firms of solicitors and individual barristers who have considerable expertise in this area.

LEVELS OF FUNDING

There are two broad categories of funding in civil cases: 'Initial Legal Help' and 'Higher levels of funding'. Initial Legal Help covers the cost of getting advice from a solicitor. It is available to those whose disposable income is no more than £649 a month and whose disposable capital is no more than £8,000. More funding may be available if, for instance, the case is going to court. This will depend on the chances of the case succeeding and the means of the applicant. The means limits for the higher levels of funding are higher than for Initial Legal Help.

Legal aid reform: current issues

For the last few years, the government has been concerned at the increase in the volume of legal aid cases and the related costs. They commissioned Lord Carter to review the system, in consultation with the legal profession, and to make recommendations as to the reform of the legal aid system.

In 2006, Lord Carter produced his report: 'Legal Aid: A market-based approach to reform', which made radical suggestions for overhauling the system. Following this, the DCA and LSC issued a consultation paper and then a Command paper: 'Legal Aid Reform: The Way Ahead'. This broadly accepts Lord Carter's reforms and has proposed a market-based system, with price-competitive tendering for legal aid contracts, and fixed fees for legal work rather than hourly rates.

These proposals have caused outrage in the legal community. One reason for this is that the tendering process will mean that many smaller legal firms will close – the Law Society even estimated even 800 firms will be forced to close. The legal profession is also worried that fixed fee arrangements will lead to corner-cutting by legal firms.

The Constitutional Affairs Committee in May 2007 echoed some of these concerns, and suggested that the reforms may leave the most vulnerable groups in society at risk in terms of access to justice. It also raised concerns over the impact on ethnic minority firms, which tend to be smaller and therefore more at risk.

In September 2010 the Law Society brought an action for judicial review of the legality of the tendering process in relation to the family law contract by the Legal Services Commission (*R (Law Society of England and Wales) v the Legal Services Commission* (Case Number CO/9207/10)). The High Court held that tender round was unlawful and severely hindered access to justice for vulnerable children and their parents. The LSC subsequently decided not to appeal the decision. In October 2010, the Justice Secretary was reported to be considering the closure of up to 157 courts to reduce the £1.1 billion spent on the courts system and to make savings in legal aid of £350 million by 2014. Nicholas Green QC, Chairman of the Bar Council, said that these cuts were 'brutal' and that access to justice should be the first priority.

CRIMINAL DEFENCE SERVICE

The Criminal Defence Service (CDS) replaced the old system of criminal legal aid on 2 April 2001. The Access to Justice Act 1999 states that the CDS was created:

> For the purpose of securing that individuals involved in criminal investigations or criminal proceedings have access to such advice, assistance and representation as the interests of justice require.

The CDS is run by the LSC, but it is an entirely separate scheme from the CLS, with a separate budget. The Commission enters into contracts with legal service providers for different types of criminal defence services. All contracts include quality requirements and prices are usually fixed in advance. Fixed prices provide an incentive to avoid delay, and reward efficient practice. Opponents of the system, however, have argued that fixed-price work is not conducive to justice, and encourages corner-cutting. If a case requires the services of a specialist advocate in the Crown Court, this is usually covered by a separate contract.

Very complex and expensive cases – where the trial is expected to last 41 days or more – are not covered by ordinary contracts. A defendant's choice of solicitor is limited to firms on a specialist panel, and a separate contract will be agreed in each case.

As of 2 April 2001, solicitors in private practice can only carry out criminal defence work for the CDS if they have a 'General Criminal Contract' (GCC). Firms can apply for a crime category franchise, and will be awarded one if they pass an audit by the LSC. There are three types of GCC: the 'All Classes' contract, the Prison Law contract and the Criminal Cases Review Commission contract.

There are two ways in which an individual can be helped by the CDS: 'Advice and Assistance', and 'Representation'.

ADVICE AND ASSISTANCE

Advice and Assistance covers help from a solicitor, including giving general advice, writing letters, negotiating, getting a barrister's opinion and preparing a written case. It is means tested, and the current level under which a person will qualify is £95 per week in disposable income, and from £1,000 in disposable capital. In some instances separate 'Advocacy Assistance' will be appropriate. This covers the cost of a solicitor preparing a case and initial representation in the magistrates' or the Crown Court. It also covers representation in some prison law cases.

REPRESENTATION

Representation is available for those charged with a criminal offence, and is granted by application to the magistrates' court. It covers the cost of a solicitor to prepare a defence before going to court, and to provide representation. It may also be available for bail applications. If the case requires a barrister, then those fees are also covered. It can also cover advice on appeal against verdict or sentence.

The Criminal Defence Service Act 2006 changed the system by which applicants could qualify for criminal legal aid. There is now a 2 stage process:

1   as under the old system, the applicant must pass an 'interests of justice' test – sometimes called a 'merits test'. It will usually be in the interests of justice to grant representation where a custodial sentence is likely, or where there are substantial questions of law to be argued;
2   if the applicant passes the first stage, he will then have to take a means test. This will see if he is financially eligible for legal aid, by looking at his income and expenditure (but not capital).

The Government's rationale is that those who can afford to pay for their defence costs should be made to do so and that legal aid resources should be targeted towards those who need them most.

DUTY SOLICITOR SCHEMES

Duty solicitor schemes operate in police stations, and the magistrates' and Crown Courts. The solicitor on duty is there to give legal advice to those who require it quickly, and without means testing.

Recently, a Public Defender Service (PDS) has been established. There are 4 regional offices. This provides a salaried provider of criminal defenders. The LSC employs PDS staff, who provide independent advice, assistance and representation on criminal matters.

In an independent report evaluating the effectiveness of the PDS, researchers concluded that it was generally working. It said that the PDS had a very important role to play in:

- providing protection against the market concentration and instability that may result from a system of competitive tendering for defence services;

- as a guarantee of client choice and quality in criminal defence services; and

- in supporting future service improvement and innovation in this field.

ALTERNATIVE LEGAL SERVICES

COMMUNITY LEGAL ADVICE CENTRES AND NETWORKS

The LSC is aiming to integrate two main areas of its work (family and social welfare) and set up a system of community legal advice centres (single centres) and networks (groups of providers). The centres and networks will be publicly funded, by the LSC and local councils. Providers have to compete by tender and are awarded a contract to run the centre/network. The intention is that every centre and network will provide advice and representation in:

- community care

- debt

- employment

- family

- housing

- welfare benefits

- any public law relating to these categories.

They will also provide general advice and identify opportunities for tackling common causes of local problems. Some of the aims of the centres are as follows:

- they will enable people to protect their fundamental rights and sort out legal disputes;

- they will assist in tackling disadvantage and promoting social inclusion;

- they will deliver legal advice services to local communities according to local needs and priorities;

- they will provide quality integrated legal advice services.

The first of these centres opened in Gateshead in 2007 and others are planned around the country.

LEGAL ADVICE CENTRES

Normally found in Citizens' Advice Bureaux or universities; lawyers give free advice, usually regarding areas of welfare law.

CITIZENS' ADVICE BUREAUX

The workers in the Citizens' Advice Bureaux are usually trained in dealing with clients' problems, of which a great number are legally based.

LAW CENTRES

These were established in 1968 by the Society of Labour Lawyers in *Justice For All*. They were established to:

- educate the public in their rights and duties under the law; and

- specialise in specific areas of law which were seen as appropriate to poorer sections of the community, such as landlord and tenant, employment law and social security law.

You should now be confident that you would be able to tick all of the boxes on the checklist at the beginning of this chapter. To check your knowledge of Access to justice why not visit the companion website and take the Multiple Choice Question test. Check your understanding of the terms and vocabulary used in this chapter with the flashcard glossary.

Putting it into practice...

Now that you've mastered the basics, you will want to put it all into practice. The Routledge Questions and Answers series provides an ideal opportunity for you to apply your understanding and knowledge of the law and to hone your essay-writing technique.

We've included one exam-style essay question, which replicates the type of question posed in the Routledge Questions and Answers series to give you some essential exam practice. The Q&A includes an answer plan and a fully worked model answer to help you recognise what examiners might look for in your answer.

QUESTION 1

What are the main sources of law today?

Answer plan

This is, apparently, a very straightforward question, but the temptation is to ignore the European Community (EU) as a source of law and to overemphasise custom as a source. The following structure does not make these mistakes:

◼ in the contemporary situation, it would not be improper to start with the EU as a source of UK law;

◼ then attention should be moved on to domestic sources of law: statute and common law;

◼ the increased use of delegated legislation should be emphasised;

◼ custom should be referred to, but its extremely limited operation must be emphasised.

Answer

European law
Since the UK joined the European Economic Community (EEC) (now, following the Lisbon Treaty, the European Union (EU)), it has progressively but effectively passed the power to create laws which are operative in this country to the wider European institutions. The UK is now subject to Community law, not just as a direct consequence of the various treaties of accession passed by the UK Parliament, but increasingly, it is subject to the secondary legislation generated by the various institutions of the EU.

European law takes three distinct forms: regulations, directives and decisions. Regulations are immediately effective without the need for the UK Parliament to produce its own legislation. Directives, on the other hand, require specific legislation to implement their proposals, but the UK Parliament is under an obligation to enact such legislation as will give effect to their implementation. Decisions of the ECJ are binding throughout the EU and take precedence over any domestic law.

Parliamentary legislation

Under UK constitutional law, it is recognised that Parliament has the power to enact, revoke or alter such and any law it sees fit to deal with and no one Parliament can bind its successors. The extent of this sovereignty may be brought into question with respect to the EU for such time as the UK remains a member, but within the UK, Parliament's power is absolute. This absolute power is a consequence of the historical struggle between Parliament and the Stuart monarchy in the seventeenth century. Parliament arrogated to itself absolute law-making power, a power not challenged by the courts, which were in turn granted an independent sphere of operation. It should be remembered, however, that the Human Rights Act (HRA) 1998 has, for the first time, given the courts the power to question, although not strike down, primary legislation as being incompatible with the rights protected under the European Convention on Human Rights (ECHR). It also allows the courts to declare secondary legislation to be invalid for the same reason.

Parliament makes law in the form of legislation, that is, Acts of Parliament. There are various types of legislation. Whereas public Acts affect the public generally, private Acts only affect a limited sector of the populace, either particular people or people within a particular locality. Within the category of public Acts, a further distinction can be made between government Bills and Private Member's Bills. The former are usually introduced by the Government, whilst the latter are the product of individual initiative on the part of particular MPs.

Before enactment, the future Act is referred to as a Bill and many Bills are the product of independent commissions, such as the Law Commission, or committees, such as the Law Reform Committee and the Criminal Law Revision Committee. Without going into the details of the procedure, Bills have to be considered by both Houses of Parliament and have to receive Royal Assent before they are actually enacted.

Delegated legislation has to be considered as a source of law, in addition, but subordinate, to general Acts of Parliament. Generally speaking, delegated legislation is law made by some person or body to whom Parliament has delegated its general law-making power. In statistical terms, it is arguable that at present, delegated legislation is actually more significant than primary Acts of Parliament. The output of delegated legislation in any year greatly exceeds the output of Acts of Parliament and, each year, there are over 3,000 sets of rules and regulations made in the form of delegated legislation, compared to fewer than 100 public Acts of Parliament. Delegated legislation can take the form of Orders in Council, which permit the Government to make law through the Privy Council. This power is usually considered in relation to impending emergencies, but perhaps its widest effect is to be found in relation to EU law, for under s 2(2) of the European Communities Act 1972, ministers can give effect to provisions of the Community which do not have direct effect. Most delegated legislation, however, takes the form of statutory instruments, through which government ministers exercise the powers given to them by general enabling legislation to make the particular rules which are to apply to any given situation within its ambit. A third type of delegated legislation is the bylaw, through which local authorities and public bodies are able to make legally binding rules within their area of competence or authority.

Delegated legislation has developed for a number of reasons. One such reason is the increased pressure on Parliamentary time, with the consequent hiving off of detailed and time-consuming work to ministers and their specialist departments. Another reason for the growth in the output of delegated legislation is the highly technical nature of the subject matter to which it tends to be addressed and the concomitant need for such rules themselves to be highly technical. Any piece of delegated legislation is only valid if it is within the ambit of the powers actually delegated by Parliament. Any law made outside that restricted ambit of authority is void, as being *ultra vires*, and is open to challenge in the courts under the process of judicial review.

Common law

The next source of law that has to be considered is case law, the effective creation and refinement of law in the course of judicial decisions. It should be remembered that the UK's law is still a common law system and, even if legislation in its various guises is of ever increasing importance, the significance and effectiveness of judicial creativity should not be discounted. Judicial decisions are a source of law, through the operation of the doctrine of judicial precedent. This process depends on the established hierarchy of the courts and operates in such a way that generally, a court is bound by the *ratio decidendi*, or rule of law implicit in the decision of a court above it in the hierarchy and usually by a court of equal standing in that hierarchy. Where statute law does not cover a particular area, or where the law is silent, it will be generally necessary for a court deciding cases relating to such an area to determine what the law is and, in so doing, that court will inescapably and unarguably be creating law. The scope for judicial creativity should not be underestimated and it should be remembered that the task of interpreting the actual meaning of legislation in particular cases also falls to the judiciary and provides it with a further important area of discretionary creativity. As the highest court in the land, the Supreme Court has particular scope for creating or extending the common law, and a relatively contemporary example of its adopting such an active stance can be seen in the way in which it overruled the long-standing presumption that a man could not be guilty of the crime of rape against his wife (see *R* [1991]). It should, of course, always be remembered that Parliament remains sovereign as regards the creation of law and any aspect of the judicially created common law is subject to direct alteration by statute.

An extension of the doctrine of judicial precedent leads to a consideration of a further possible source of law, for when the court is unable to locate a precise or analogous precedent, it may refer to legal textbooks for guidance and assistance. Such books are sub-divided, depending on when they were written. In strict terms, only certain venerable works of antiquity are actually treated as authoritative sources of law. Amongst the most important of these works are those by Glanvill from the twelfth century, Bracton from the thirteenth century, Coke from the seventeenth century and Blackstone from the eighteenth century. Legal works produced after *Blackstone's Commentaries of 1765* are considered to be of recent origin, but although they cannot be treated as authoritative sources, the courts on occasion will look at the most eminent works by accepted experts in particular fields in order to help determine what the law is or should be.

Custom

The final source of law that remains to be considered is custom. The romantic view of the common law is that it represented a crystallisation of common customs, distilled by the judiciary in the course of its travels around the land. Although some of the common law may have had its basis in general custom, a large proportion of these so-called customs were invented by the judges themselves and represented what they wanted the law to be, rather than what people generally thought it was.

There is, however, a second possible customary source of law and that is rules derived from specific local customs. Here, there is the possibility that the local custom might differ from the common law and thus limit its operation. Even in this respect, however, reliance on customary law as opposed to common law, although not impossible, is made unlikely by the stringent test that any appeal to it has to satisfy. Amongst these requirements are that the custom must have existed from 'time immemorial' (that is, since 1189) and must have been exercised continuously within that period and without opposition. The custom must also have been felt as obligatory, have been consistent with other customs and, in the final analysis, must be reasonable. Given this list of requirements, it can be seen why local custom does not loom large as an important source of law.

Common Pitfall

The temptation is to concentrate on only one source such as legislation or the common law and to go into far more detail than is necessary for such a general question. Remember that each subtopic in this answer can be asked as a question topic in its own right. So remember to cover most if not all of the potential sources.

AIM HIGHER

It is essential to be aware of the EU as a source of modern law and reference to the Lisbon Treaty will show an up to date awareness of that particular source.In relation to legislation, reference could be made to examples of legislation introduced by the new coalition government.